The World of SMURFS

A CELEBRATION OF TINY BLUE PROPORTIONS

by Matt. Murray

The World of SMURFS

A CELEBRATION OF TINY BLUE PROPORTIONS

by Matt. Murray

ABRAMS IMAGE | NEW YORK

CONTENTS

INTRODUCTION

Greetings, Blue Believers!
And welcome to *The World of Smurfs!*

WHILE THERE'S NO one book that can *completely* encapsulate the entirety of the Smurfs' history, this book has been written and designed to serve as a tourists' guide to lead you through what has been fifty-plus years of comics, cartoons, memorabilia, and memories that could fill a village.

To some who just remember The Smurfs as an animated cartoon they curled up to watch on Saturday mornings—a bowl of Smurfberry Crunch in one hand and their stuffed Smurfette in the other—some of the information and images we've assembled may come as a surprise. Indeed, when I embarked upon my studies to become a self-proclaimed "Smurfologist" back in 2005, much of the Smurfs' back-story seemed as foreign to me as the French it was written in.

I grew up in New York City during the 1980s, and was just the right age to go completely smurfy when the series premiered in September 1981. I watched the show every week, often getting into fights with my older brother to keep control of the family television set into the second half-hour, as he usually wanted to turn the channel to something else. (He liked

The Smurfs, too. He just wanted to turn it off because I loved them.) My parents rewarded me for good grades with little plastic Smurfs, and I was extra excited on the birthday I received a Papa Smurf Mushroom Cottage. I had the books, the pencil sharpeners, the belt buckle, the wind-up toys . . . If I ever had a favorite color before Smurf blue, I wouldn't have told you then and I couldn't tell you now. I was a fluent speaker of Smurf, and they were often the only topic of conversation that would engage me. As a result, my maternal grandmother had to become a weekly viewer of the program as well, so that: a) we could have something to talk about on the phone; and b) she could understand the actual words I was smurfing.

In time, I thought I had grown out of them; The Smurfs became just a memory, a cartoon I'd watched when I was younger.

It wasn't until I was assembling a museum exhibit on Saturday morning cartoons, which explored not only the art but the social, political, and economic effects of specific shows, that I took another good look at The Smurfs. Those early memories came back to me and what I saw was not just a cartoon that I watched

when I was younger, but something that, in some way, had affected almost every member of my family. The more informal research I did leading up to the exhibit, the more I found that I wasn't the only person with stories like these. People from all over the United States, Canada, South America, the UK, France, and Belgium (the Smurfs' homeland) had personal tales about our old blue buddies.

It led me to ask: What was it about these little blue leprechauns that brought families together, smiles to faces, and entertained everyone from three to sixty-three (and no doubt beyond)?

The answer, I thought, would lie in the material itself. Over time I had developed a vague notion that the Smurfs had a life before the cartoon, so I began to dig into that history. What I discovered was decades' worth of stories, toys, comics, articles, animated cartoons, references, and memories—many of which had never even made it to the shores of my country, the great pop cultural juggernaut of the world. I found myself completely humbled by it and a bit overwhelmed, considering that I only had about fifteen square inches of wall space at the gallery to discuss the entire phenomenon, and it had to

be through the filter of the cartoon. Not nearly enough physical or meta-physical space to answer the question: Just what is it about those Smurfs?

Years later, with the exhibit mounted and long since closed, I'm still not sure I can answer that question. I'm not even sure if there's a definite answer. It's magical, elusive, much like the Smurfs themselves . . . and I've looked everywhere. I've watched all of the 272 episodes of the cartoon series (in Europe there are only 256, as the sixteen Johan and Peewit segments are considered their own show); read most of the dozens of comic "albums" in the original French (and some in multiple languages); and I've even restarted my long-abandoned collection of Smurfs figurines, filling in the gaps with the ones I desperately wanted as a kid but never got, ones that I never knew existed because they were available only in Europe, and the new ones that have been released in recent years.

The Smurfs' 50th Anniversary in 2008 was a fine time to be a Smurfologist or even a casual fan in America, as we saw a Smurf take to the skies as a balloon in the Macy's Thanksgiving Day Parade and heard rumblings about a Smurfs theatrical movie, the first in three

decades. All of this of course has been, and is, creating new generations of fans, some of whom I hope will pick up the mantle of exploring the history behind the Smurfs and will go on to call themselves "Smurfologists" one day.

Maybe one of them will be able to answer the question: Just what is it about those Smurfs?

I hope this book is helpful to them, and to you, as an introduction to, or refresher course on, what it is that has us asking that question, and what it is that brings us back, again and again, to the world of Smurfs.

—Matt. Murray, Smurfologist

P.S. *If you find, or already have the answer, give me a call. Like my grandma before me, I've smurfed up on smurfing the language.*

THE SMURFS' PAPA

Peyo

Pierrot le Jeune

WHEN SEEN ON the cover of a book or at the beginning of a cartoon, the word can seem like a magical incantation that can spirit you away to another world . . . and it is.

But it's hard to believe that it was simply a man's name. Of British and Walloon (Belgian) descent, Pierre Culliford got the name Peyo from an English-speaking cousin who had trouble pronouncing Pierrot, the French nickname for Pierre.

Culliford would use it as his cartoonist nom de plume, and his famous monograph would inspire Smurfs fans the world over to ask: What, or rather who, was Peyo?

Pierre Culliford was born on June 25, 1928, in Brussels, Belgium. The youngest child of Richard Culliford, an investment banker, and Marguerite Kulinckx, Pierre had a brother, Walter, and sister, Lucienne. An athletic boy, he especially enjoyed gymnastics, and while he excelled at physical education at school, he was far from a model student.

He opened his textbooks mainly to draw in them. The only class he enjoyed was history, as the stories of bygone eras provided a playground for his vast imagination. His very first comic panels were scrawled in the borders of his history book and starred the likes of Julius Caesar. While his mother

was encouraging of Pierre's penchant for art, she disapproved of his early disregard for the formal education system.

Although he hated sitting through lectures, young Pierre was fond of giving them. Every week, his extended family would come over to his house and, while the adults would chitchat around the dinner table, Pierre and the children would adjourn to the library where he would recount his favorite tales from history. As he grew more interested in the comics section of newspapers and magazines, Pierre expanded his repertoire to include performances of the latest adventures from popular strips such as Tintin and Mickey Mouse.

In 1935, Richard Culliford passed away after a two-year struggle with an illness that could not be properly diagnosed by the medical practices of the time. While the family was provided for through Richard's wise investments, Marguerite Culliford lacked her husband's business acumen and misspent the bulk of the money within a few years of becoming a widow.

Despite changing neighborhoods and schools, Pierre remained an outgoing child, finding joy in entertaining people. He acted in school plays and

LEFT | (TOP) The Culliford Family, 1929. From left to right: Walter, Marguerite, Pierre, Richard, and Lucienne. (BOTTOM) Pierre, age four. **PREVIOUS** | Marguerite Culliford with her youngest child, Pierre, in 1929.

sang in the choir. He was also a member of the Catholic Boy Scouts, which continued to encourage his athleticism. While he still liked to draw, he never focused on creating "fine art," preferring to sketch in a more cartoonish style. As is the case with most people destined to be recognized as geniuses in their field, he even failed certain assignments in art class. He had at least one teacher tell him that he "had no future in drawing." That didn't stop him from creating caricatures of his teachers or crafting rudimentary comic strips, but most of his attention was devoted to either acting or singing.

The Nazi occupation of Belgium would find Marguerite relocating her children to her family home in Schaerbeek, Belgium, in May of 1940. At only twelve years old, Pierre was too young to fully understand what was going on in the world around him. He celebrated bombings, as they meant days off from school, which he still despised.

After finishing sixth grade, Pierre was enrolled in a trade school with the hope that he would learn a vocation. Showing no inherent skills as a rough tradesman, he was forced to repeat the first year and dropped out during the second. He tried to enroll in a more

RIGHT | (TOP) Pierre (forming his own top row) with his school choral group in 1938. (BOTTOM) Pierre practices technical drawing at College Cardinal c. 1942–43.

La Compagnie Belge d'Actualités

During the Nazi occupation, Belgium's doors of cultural exchange were closed to the world, allowing no information in or out of the country without German approval. Similarly, the Nazis kept an eye on material produced for distribution inside Belgium, replacing proper news agencies and entertainment distributors with pieces of their own propaganda machine.

No longer able to produce cinematic newsreels, Paul Nagant, director of la Compagnie Belge d'Actualités (C.B.A.)—the Belgian News Company—decided to use his resources to make animated short films. To help him, Nagant hired two animators fresh out of art school: Eddy Paape and Jacques Eggermont. Inspired by the Disney Studios, the company chose to adapt fairy tales and folk music.

After a fire burned down its studio in Liege, the C.B.A. moved to Brussels and, after the 1944 Liberation, the studio decided to expand and hire more artists. The 1945 roster of animators and staff included the likes of Maurice De Bevere (aka Morris) and Andre Franquin, who took what they perceived to be "steady" jobs in animation while they pursued careers in comics.

Though the company had the ambition to grow and a stable of young talent, many of its projects never made it out of the development stage. With the end of the war, the European market was flooded with insanely popular American animated films from larger, better-funded studios such as Disney and Warner Bros. The C.B.A.'s short films didn't stand a chance against the return of Mickey Mouse and the appearance of the Looney Tunes.

By 1946, the small Belgian studio had gone bankrupt and had to shut down, but the animation world's minor loss would be the comics world's gain, as a number of those cartoonists would usher in a golden age of Belgian comics during the 1950s and 1960s.

academic school, but found the other students more advanced than he, and, again, dropped out.

At fifteen, Pierre was forced to enter the adult world and find a job. A film lover, he took a job as an assistant projectionist at a local movie house. While he hated the German propaganda of the newsreels he ran, he relished the opportunity to watch free movies. Ultimately, he found the actual work (the spooling and rewinding of reels in a cramped closet for hours on end) tedious, and, as it was a solitary job, he sought camaraderie in the friends he had made as a scout.

After two years, Pierre was feeling fed up with the low-paying life of a projectionist. For side work, he performed numerous odd jobs—like decorating lampshades, which did engage his artistic abilities—but he was completely unsatisfied with life as he knew it. One day, he decided to comb the classifieds. Two ads caught his eye—one was for a dental assistant, the other was to apprentice at a small animation studio formed by la Compagnie Belge d'Actualités.

He went to the dentist's office to find that the position had been filled just minutes before his arrival, leaving the C.B.A. as his only hope of getting out of the projection booth.

OPPOSITE | Pierre (on the right) working as a cel painter at the C.B.A. **RIGHT |** Young Pierre on the streets of Brussels c. 1946.

"J'arriverai!"

In 1945 the C.B.A. hired seventeen-year-old Pierre Culliford for its ink-and-paint department—much to the young artist's surprise—but the work wouldn't last long. Within months of his hiring, the C.B.A. shut down and Pierre lost his job. While some animators would find work at the Belgian comics anthology, *Le Journal Spirou*, the editors found Pierre's work to be weaker than the others and didn't hire him.

In order to build his drafting skills, he began studying at the Académie Royale des Beaux-Arts, but after three months he found himself more interested in socializing than sitting through drawing classes. During this time, he would meet one girl in particular who would capture his heart, Janine "Nine" Devroye. The two would date for close to five years before finally getting married on June 9, 1951.

During those five years, Pierre completely dedicated himself to getting a job as an artist. Most of his work came in advertising: drawing ads for local shops or logos for paper shopping bags. All the while, he never gave up his aspirations to become a cartoonist with his own comic strip in the Sunday comic supplements

LEFT | In November 1946, Pierre met Janine Devroye through a mutual friend. The two dated for nearly five years before getting married.

of newspapers or in the pages of magazines like *Spirou*, or *Le Journal Tintin*, which began publishing after the war.

In 1946 Pierre managed to sell a few short stories about the Indian warrior Pied-Tendre (Tenderfoot) and his scout Puce (Chip) to the comics section of *L'Occident*. That same year, *Bon Marché* bought a Tintin-inspired comic called "Une aventure de l'inspecteur Pik" for its *Le Petit Monde* supplement; and *La Dernière Heure* would pick up the first installments of Johan, an adventure strip about a medieval page boy. By this point he had begun to sign his work "Peyo," and while he hadn't necessarily made a proper name for himself, his now-famous signature had begun to take shape.

Although he failed to sell other adventure strips, like the pirate saga *Capitaine Coky*, Culliford still managed to find steady advertising work while trying to develop more comics. In 1949, he noticed a trend toward funny animals and created *Poussy*, a gag strip about a cat, which was purchased by *Le Soir*. A success, *Poussy* led to the newspaper picking up further adventures of Johan from the artist, and both comics would enjoy long runs in that paper.

RIGHT | Rare color work done by Peyo in the late 1940s. (CLOCK-WISE FROM LEFT) A 1949 cover for the magazine *Le Moustique*, his first work for Dupuis; an early panel illustration of Poussy (also 1949); and a 1947 cartoon depicting a camping trip taken with Nine, who is shown at the head of the pack.

The Marcinelle School

Located in the town of Marcinelle, Belgium, Spirou's editorial office became the epicenter of an artistic movement that would shake up the Belgian comics scene and drive the rivalry between its magazine and *Le Journal Tintin*, which opened its offices in Brussels, Belgium.

Led by Joseph Gillain (aka Jijé), L'École de Marcinelle (the Marcinelle School), drew in a highly stylized manner that would be called *comique-dynamique* (humorous dynamism) that emphasized character and movement and contrasted with the straightforward and more realistic *ligne claire* style that was instituted by Hergé in the pages of Tintin (both the comic and the magazine later named for it).

During the occupation, Jijé was one of the few cartoonists who not only kept his job, but also expanded his output when he was hired to fill the pages left blank by the embargo on foreign strips. In addition to creating *Freddy Fred*, *Jean Valhardi*, and *Blondin et Cirage*, Jijé was hired to draw territory-specific versions of Superman and Red Ryder and took over the illustration of Spirou's title strip, which was originally drawn by a Frenchman who signed his work Rob-Vel.

Following World War II, there was a boom in the Belgian publishing industry as the country again tried to find its own voice. As Jijé's workload became too much for one man to handle, he hired a team of assistants who moved into his Waterloo home and would become the champions of the Marcinelle School: Franquin, Morris, Eddy Paape, and Will (real name: Willy Maltaite).

This crew, who came to be known as the "Gang of Four," were tutored by Jijé in how to draw in his style before taking over his popular comic strips, and that influence remained evident in their own work when they went on to create their own groundbreaking characters such as Marsupilami, Gaston Lagaffe (both Franquin), and Lucky Luke (Morris).

As their popularity grew, the Gang's own influence would be felt and seen in the work of other Belgian artists including Peyo, who would later infuse the comic-dynamic style into the work of his own assistants and members of his studio.

Johan (and Pirlouit)

Though this was a financially trying time for the artist, he never let poverty distract him from his goal of being an established cartoonist. His motto during this period was *J'arriverai!* (comparable to the English idiom "I'm gonna make it!"), and his hope kept him personally and professionally afloat.

Although he continued to submit samples to the major magazines, his comics went largely ignored by their editors, until a colleague from his days at the C.B.A. opened a door for him in the offices of *Spirou*.

A chance encounter with *Spirou*'s superstar, André Franquin, would get Peyo hired at the magazine.

Though the two hadn't really spoken since their time at the C.B.A. and despite thinking that Peyo still had some progress to make as an artist, Franquin respected Peyo's enthusiasm and drive to make it in the industry. On Franquin's recommendation, Charles Dupuis, publisher of *Spirou*, hired Peyo in 1952. The artist brought Johan over to the magazine, but the comic would have to be revised before it would see publication.

OPPOSITE | (TOP) Peyo, third from left, with colleagues. (BOTTOM) From left, Fournier, Franquin, Peyo, and Tillieux share a toast. **RIGHT |** Peyo's early promotional artwork for Johan, done in 1947, presented in front of later finished pages from Poussy and Johan et Pirlouit created by Peyo's studio of artists.

First, Johan himself received a makeover. A blond page boy in his early teens, the character would be remodeled into dark-haired young man in the early days of his knighthood. Next, the scope of his adventures would have to be broadened and the length of his tales expanded to fit the scale of Spirou's running strips. Originally serialized in half-page weekly installments for *Le Soir*, Johan's stories would have to be told in full-page format and would, when collected, have to amount to forty-four full pages in order to fill an "album" (a large-format storybook comprising a complete adventure, or a collection of short ones) that could later be published and sold by Dupuis.

While Peyo first felt daunted by the task of creating long-form comics, Franquin was there to guide him through the process. Daily conversations and critiques from the established cartoonist helped Peyo expand his storytelling horizons. By serving as his assistant on some of Franquin's other work, Peyo's art style and composition improved greatly. With the steady work Spirou provided, Peyo was able to encourage his new bride, Nine, to leave her job as a bank clerk to serve as his personal assistant and colorist.

OPPOSITE | On the far left is the original 1956 cover for the album *Le Lutin du Bois aux Roches* (*The Goblin of Rocky Wood*), which featured the debut of Pirlouit. **RIGHT |** The first series of *Johan* strips created in 1947, as well as preliminary character studies of the strip's primary cast (RIGHT and OPPOSITE). Note the younger, blond appearance of Johan at the top of this page.

As Peyo grew more comfortable, Johan began to push the boundaries of straightforward medieval adventure, and took on aspects of other genres including detective fiction and fantasy. After two full solo outings ("Le Châtiment de Basenhau" in 1952 and "Le Maître de Roucybeuf" in 1953), Johan was given a sidekick, allowing for an element of humor in the comic.

Originally believed to be an apple-stealing, practical-joke-playing goblin that haunted the nearby woods, Pirlouit emerged in the pages of 1954's "Le Lutin du bois aux roches" and quickly stole the hearts of the readers. A little person with a huge mouth and a knack for getting into trouble, Pirlouit proved to be an excellent contrast to the somber and serious Johan, and his popularity earned him a place in the title of the series, which had helped drive Spirou's sales to 80,000 copies a week in Belgium and 108,000 copies in France—great circulation for a European magazine in 1954.

To cement his success and show his versatility, Peyo resurrected Poussy as a short gag strip in the pages of Spirou, and he soon found himself being contacted for other work outside of

LEFT | (TOP) An early draft of a page from "Le Châtiment de Basenhau" ("The Punishment of Basenhau," 1952), Johan's first adventure illustrated for the pages of Spirou, and a portrait of the artist taken in the same era. (BOTTOM) An early depiction of Johan and Pirlouit from the early 1950s. **OPPOSITE** | The characters' more familiar stylization, which was standardized by the publication of "La Flèche noire" ("The Black Arrow") in 1957.

Spirou, but he didn't abandon Johan et Pirlouit. Between 1955 and 1958 he crafted stories of varying lengths for Spirou, from the full-length sagas "La Pierre de lune" ("The Moonstone") and "La Flèche noire" ("The Black Arrow") to the short stories "Le Dragon vert" ("The Green Dragon") and "La Veillée de Noël" ("Christmas Eve.") "La Flûte à six trous" ("The Flute with Six Holes"), a full-length adventure begun in the pages of Spirou no. 1047 (May 8, 1958), would turn out to be an important one, although the reason wouldn't become evident until more than midway through the storyline (no. 1071, October 23, 1958.) In the tale, Pirlouit finds a magic flute that causes all those who hear it to lose control and dance themselves into a frenzy. When the flute falls into villainous hands, Johan and Pirlouit are sent on a quest to find the makers of the flute, as only they can break the spell. Those special artisans would be "les Schtroumpfs."

LEFT | Published color pages from the *Johan et Pirlouit* adventures "Le Pays maudit" ("The Cursed Land," 1961, left) and "Le Serment des Vikings" ("The Vikings' Oath," 1955, right).

Les Schtroumpfs

A tribe of little leprechauns who lived in the Cursed Land, the Schtroumpfs actually had their origin in an animated cartoon Peyo was working on at the C.B.A., before the studio's closing stopped production. The short film, *Un Cadeau à la fée* (*The Fairy's Gift*), was to feature a race of dancing pink elves clad in pointed caps made of flower petals.

Starting with that design, Peyo began to craft his new breed of magical imps, but he believed a pink color scheme would make them look too human. As his colorist, Peyo's wife would help him overcome that obstacle. It was a simple process of elimination for Nine: As they were to live in a forest surrounded by foliage, the characters would disappear into the background if they were green; as green's opposing color, red would make them stand out too much; yellow is considered to be unlucky, so that wouldn't work; in her mind, that left only blue.

To further differentiate these elves from his human characters, Peyo decided they should speak their own language. For that piece of the puzzle he again reached back to a prior experience, but this was from a more recent memory.

RIGHT | Young Pierre Culliford's character studies for the unproduced short film *Un Cadeau à la fée*, c. 1946.

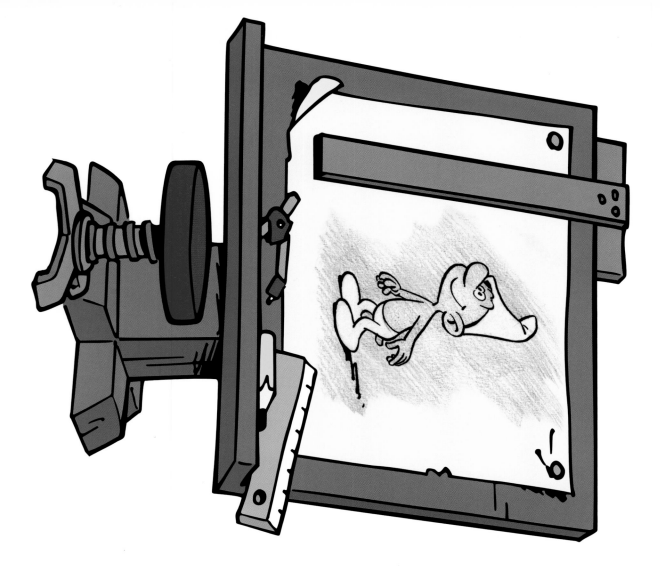

In 1957, flush with the success of their comic strips Peyo, Franquin, and their families (both now had children) rented a vacation home in the town of Saint-Idesbald on the Belgian coast. One night at dinner, Peyo wanted Franquin to pass him the salt but he fumbled for the words and instead asked his friend to pass him the "schtroumpf." The word was gibberish, a malapropism, but the two got such a kick out of it that they spent their time finding new ways to inject it in their everyday conversation as a noun, verb, or adjective.

"Les Schtroumpfs" were born, but to keep them mysterious, Peyo wouldn't introduce them right away. He would have them shadow Johan and Pirlouit throughout the beginning of the tale, showing their shrouded eyes in some panels or a blue hand reaching out from behind some leaves in another. It wasn't until the wizard Homnibus sends the knight and his squire to the Cursed Land via the power of "hypno-kinesis" that the duo and the reader get their first full-on Schtroumpf-ing.

Submerged in the culture and language of the Schtroumpfs, Johan and Pirlouit are both charmed and fascinated by these strange creatures. Pirlouit tries in

LEFT | Peyo's first official drawing of a Schtroumpf. From the tip of his hat to the point on his tail, the influence of the fairies from *Un Cadeau à la fée* is evident. **RIGHT |** Johan and Pirlouit's first encounter with the Schtroumpfs and the first appearance of le Grand Schtroumpf from "La Flûte à six trous" (1958).

" . . . [Franquin] responded, 'Look, here's the schtroumpf, and when you've finished schtroumpfing, schtroumpf it back to me!' It was so fun to schtroumpf for the few days we spent together, it became a joke for us."

—Peyo

vain to learn to speak "Schtroumpf," allowing for some comical moments to break up the action, and ultimately the Schtroumpfs and the humans are able to work together to beat the villain and restore life to normal.

Like Pirlouit before them, the Schtroumpfs were a huge success delivered in a small package. Popular demand had them appearing in the next Johan et Pirlouit adventure, "La Guerre des sept fontaines" (1959), and that same year the little blue gnomes were tapped to help kick off a new publishing initiative from Spirou, "mini-récits."

A self-folding supplement to be removed from the pages of Spirou, mini-récits (little stories) gave readers a

LEFT | (TOP) Peyo c. the mid-1950s, just prior to the vacation that would birth the word "Schtroumpf." (BOTTOM) Panels taken from the 1959 mini-récit "Le Voleur de Schtroumpfs" ("The Smurfnapper").

fully contained forty-eight-page story in a postcard-sized comic. Yvan Delporte, who had recently been installed as Editor-in-Chief, recognized that the diminutive stature of the Schtroumpfs made them the perfect stars for these mini-comics. Dupuis approached Peyo about the idea, and he agreed, on the condition that Delporte help him write the comic.

Their first effort, "Les Schtroumpfs noirs," had the Schtroumpfs battling themselves as the village fell victim to a disease caused by a sting from a "Bzz" fly. A basic allegory for the Black Plague that spread through Europe during the Middle Ages, "Les Schtroumpfs noirs" helped establish the basic setting and some of the original characters that would become the staples of the series, and introduced Delporte's role as a collaborator in the creative process. While Peyo had ultimate control of the storylines and characters, Delporte would help develop the particulars of the plot and write the dialogue before Peyo committed the final script to paper and created the artwork. Though they had two very different personal styles and occasionally had clashing ideas, the collaboration served to strengthen the storytelling and would last for the rest of Peyo's professional career.

RIGHT | Selected pages from the mini-récit "Les Schtroumpfs noirs" (1959).

SCHTROUMPFING IT UP

AN INSTANT HIT when they appeared in the pages of Johan et Pirlouit, the Schtroumpfs were about to take Peyo on a journey that would have him transformed from an artist with a series of successful comics to a multimedia mogul with his hand in producing toys, books, and even an animated feature.

Studio Peyo

Nineteen fifty-nine not only saw the publication of the first Schtroumpfs solo story, but also the first appearance of Schtroumpf merchandise. Produced by Dupuis and sold through the pages of Spirou, a wave of two-inch latex figurines were made available to the public: a regular Schtroumpf, the wise leader "le Grand Schtroumpf," and an angry Schtroumpf that had fallen victim to the bite of the Bzz Fly.

The publisher also established TVA Dupuis, a branch dedicated to creating animated cartoons for Belgian television, and one of its first projects was an adaptation, "Les Schtroumpfs noirs." Directed by Jean Delire, the cartoon was animated using paper cutouts photographed as single frames across painted scenery, a rudimentary style popularized decades later by the creators of South Park.

Peyo was even approached by Jacques Eggermont, who remained in animation and children's entertainment after the C.B.A. closed down, about creating a puppet show inspired by the Schtroumpfs' adventures.

SPIROU 80
ALBUM du JOURNAL
DUPUIS

Unfortunately, early attempts at building the mario-nettes showed that the characters' oversized heads made the puppets too top-heavy and difficult to maneuver properly, so the project never fully materialized.

Recognizing Peyo's rising stardom, Dupuis insisted that Peyo make Poussy a full-page strip strictly for the readers of *Spirou*. The artist acquiesced, although he didn't want to completely sever his ties with *Le Soir*, the paper that gave him his early taste of success. In an effort to create a new comic for *Le Soir*, he devised Benoît Brisefer (later imported to English-speaking countries as Stephen Strong), a strip about a little boy with Herculean strength, but Dupuis liked that idea as well and purchased the comics for *Spirou*.

Peyo finally ended up selling *Jacky et Célestin* (about the adventures of two kids in Brussels) to *Le Soir*, but with five regu-lar comics to attend to, he found himself spread thin and began to amass a team of assistants to help him with his output. He stayed firmly involved with the creation and development of each property, often estab-lishing the plot and then laying out the

LEFT | (Clockwise from top) A still from a TVA Dupuis Schtroumpf television short; a character illustration of Poussy taken from a Spirou promotional poster; Benoît Brisefer bounds across the cover of a 1961 Spirou collection. **OPPOSITE** | Peyo c. 1964. **PREVIOUS** | The artist at his desk, kept company by a little blue buddy.

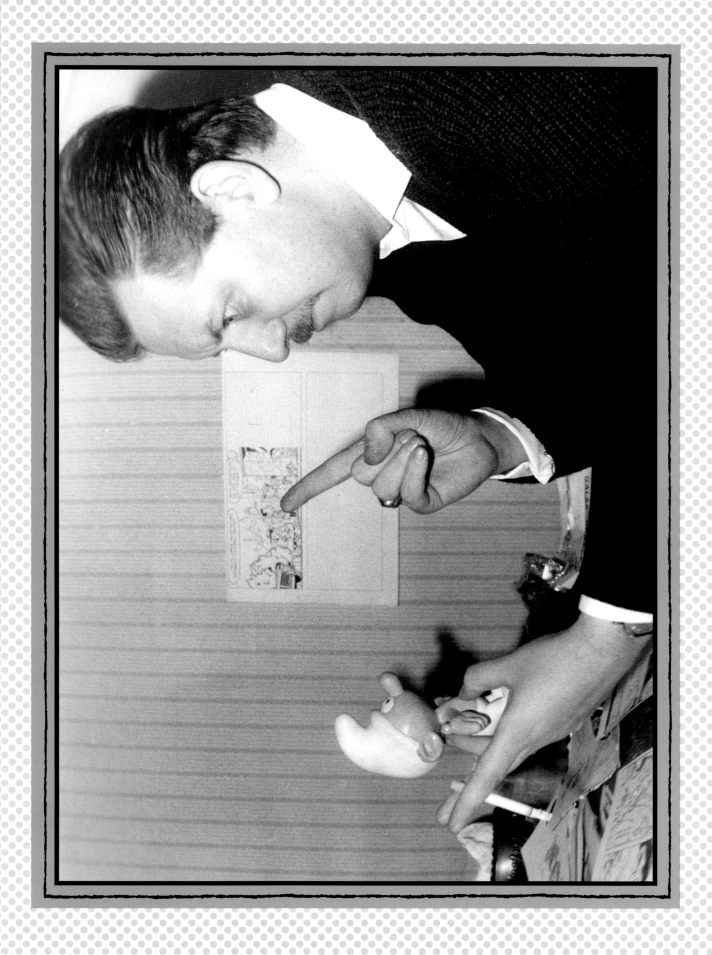

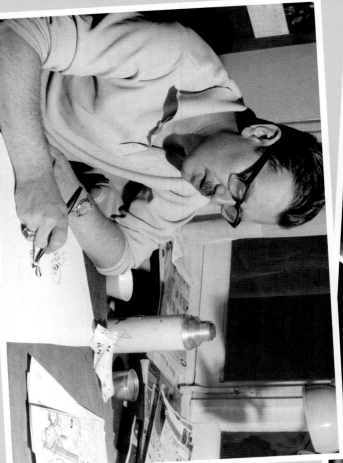

panels of any given comic before handing the work off to an assistant to fill in the details of an illustration and work with Nine on coloring before sending it out for editorial approval.

Soon Peyo found himself the head of a studio, leading a team of artists much in the way Jijé had done with the Gang of Four and the Marcinelle School. His old friend Will was handed the artistic reigns on Jacky and a rotating team of assistants—which at various points included Francis, Derib, Walthéry, Wasterlain, and Gos (who all achieved solo success later in their careers)—handled his other strips including Poussy, Benoît Brisefer, and Les Schtroumpfs. Other associates, such as Franquin, would lend an occasional hand, and, after leaving his official post at Spirou, Delporte would continue to provide written material for Peyo.

However, with the development of modern marketing and the breakout success of his characters, Pierre Culliford's role as the head of "Studio Peyo" wasn't just an artistic title but one of increasing responsibility in the selling of his creations, especially Les Schtroumpfs.

OPPOSITE | Peyo, c. 1964, laying the groundwork for the future careers of his children: Thierry (at left, born in 1956), who would grow up to write and illustrate the Smurfs comics; and Véronique (at right, born in 1958), who would eventually manage the business and marketing ends of her father's empire as the President of I.M.P.S. **LEFT** | The artist ca. 1964 (TOP) and 1967 (BOTTOM).

"Everything seemed so normal . . . I didn't realize how special it was to always have your father at home and to have all of these cartoonists in the house. They were like children themselves! Always having fun and there were unbelievable parties (that my brother and I would watch when we were supposed to be sleeping). But if there were ever any problems in either work or life, they were there for each other, like brothers."

— Veronique Culliford

Book 'em, Peyo

By 1963 *Les Schtroumpfs* had graduated from supplementary mini-comics to the prestigious pages of *Spirou* proper.

Starting with "Le Schtroumpf volant" (1963), the adventures of the Schtroumpfs had expanded from the mini-récits to the more traditional A4 single-fold-sized comics (roughly 8.5 inches by 11 inches) found in the pages of *Spirou* magazine.

Dupuis also decided to begin publishing the first Schtroumpfs comic albums, requiring the mini-récit stories to be completely redrawn by Peyo's studio to accommodate the similar upgrade in scope. As the size of the pages increased, more panels could fit on a page, which reduced the page count for each individual story and meant that more stories were required to fill each individual book.

The first book, *Les Schtroumpfs noirs* (1963), featured three tales: the title story; "Le Schtroumpf volant"; and 1959's "Le Voleur des Schtroumpfs" (*voleur* meaning thief), which introduced the villainous Gargamel and Azrael to the mix.

A lonely alchemist searching for the ingredients to make the Philosopher's Stone, Gargamel first reads

OPPOSITE | *Peyo, Nine, and their children enjoying* Les Schtroumpfs noirs *c. 1963.* **RIGHT** | *Gargamel ogles an original inked page from* Les Schtroumpfs noirs.

about the Schtroumpfs in a book of spells. He and his feline sidekick, Azrael, are successful in capturing one, but le Grand Schtroumpf (known in English as Papa) and the other Schtroumpfs band together and are able to beat their enemy. (Interestingly, Peyo's motto for the Schtroumpfs was *L'union fait la force*—or "Together we are stronger"—which is also the motto of Belgium.) Their success prompts the wizard to swear eternal vengeance on all Schtroumpf-kind. Although the Schtroumpfs would face quite a few menaces in the pages of their comics, Gargamel would become their archenemy for the life of the property.

Later in 1963, the length of the stories expanded to forty pages, and as with Johan et Pirlouit, the adventures were serialized over a string of weekly issues. The longer format allowed for more character development and the emergence of numerous Schtroumpfs from what had been relative anonymity in the blue masses.

The creation of one little Schtroumpf made quite a stir among adults and children alike. In 1966, "la Schtroumpfette" emerged from Gargamel's lab to spy on the Schtroumpf Village and possibly aid in its downfall. The Schtroumpfette creation spell, which

Je vais leur envoyer une

SCHTROUMPFETTE!

Peyo credited to his writing partner Yvan Delporte, was instantly viewed as sexist and perhaps insulting to the burgeoning feminist movement. Yet the cartoonist insisted that it was written in a spirit of fun, comparable to the songs of Jacques Brel, a Belgian songwriter who often lampooned his absolute adoration of women by celebrating what he perceived to be their stereotypical "destructive" characteristics.

Also interesting to note when reading the story is that it's Schtroumpfette's own development of a conscience and a love of Schtroumpf-kind that really turns her around. Although a spell from the Grand Schtroumpf is often cited as the reason for the Schtroumpfette's change of heart, his magic only gives her a cosmetic makeover (from brunette to blonde, plus the addition of some well-placed mascara); it's her own choice to find a way to end the discord that her presence has caused in the village. (Spoiler: she chooses to leave, but returns for later adventures!)

Nineteen sixty-six also saw the first time that Schtroumpf comics appeared outside of the pages of a Dupuis publication. That year Kellogg had brokered a deal for the Schtroumpfs to be the mascots for a number

RIGHT | "I will send them a Schtroumpfette!" According to Véronique Culliford, Peyo's assistant François Walthéry—who often pulled double duty as a babysitter—based the blonde, ultra-feminized version of the Schtroumpfette on Véronique as a five-year-old.

of their breakfast cereals in French-speaking countries. To advertise the promotion, Peyo was charged with creating full-page comic strips as advertisements. They were then run not only in Spirou, but also in the pages of their competitor Le Journal Tintin as well as in other European publications.

Three years later, the Schtroumpfs became the "spokesmen" for Biscuiteries Nantaises, a French cookie company. However, the company wasn't satisfied with just using single page comic strips to sell their product. They commissioned a full-length Schtroumpfs comic album to be sold in supermarkets that carried their product. Peyo agreed to the deal, only on the basis that he would retain the rights to the material, which could then be sold to Dupuis and reprinted in Spirou and later be redistributed as a proper part of the Schtroumpfs series sold in bookstores.

Created at breakneck speed by Peyo and his studio, Le Cosmoschtroumpf (1969) was such a hit with the fans that Kwatta set up a similar deal for the creation of L'Apprenti Schtroumpf, another comic album released in

LEFT | (TOP) Les Schtroumpfs were a popular European mascot for Kellogg products for over two decades. (BOTTOM) The cover for Les Schtroumpfs et Le Cracoucass. **OPPOSITE** | Clockwise from top: A large Papa installed to draw shoppers into a collectables shop; a "life-size" Smurf; and 5 cm and giant-size Black Smurf figures.

Gotta Schtroumpf 'em All

With what began as a modest marketing plan, Dupuis had struck gold when they started to produce two-inch latex figures of their characters, including the Schtroumpfs. While at first only three characters were available, within a few years their line of Schtroumpf collectibles came in three sizes: 5 cm (2-inch), 15 cm (about 6-inch, considered to be "life-size" for the Schtroumpfs), and the giant-size 30 cm (just under a foot high). Included were characters such as le Grand Schtroumpf and le Schtroumpfissme in addition to Johan and Pirlouit, stars of their own series but still considered part of the larger Schtroumpf universe.

Though the figures were popular with readers of Spirou and the Schtroumpfs albums, Dupuis was a publishing house that had no real interest in entering the larger toy market. As Dupuis' ability to meet the demand of the public faltered, outside companies stepped in to aid in the manufacture and distribution of the Schtroumpf figures. In 1965, the Schtroumpfs were licensed for the first time, to Schleich, a German novelty company that began making Smurf figurines in PVC (a similarly rubberlike plastic) in the same scale as the original 2-inch statuettes.

In 1966, Kellogg came knocking, looking to use the characters as mascots for their cereals. They contracted with Bully to produce a line of figures similar to those from Schleich and Dupuis that were given away with the purchase of Cornflakes and Rice Krispies. Though slightly smaller than the Dupuis and Schleich models, Bully's figurines adhered more closely to the art style then in use by Studio Peyo and became more desirable to fans and collectors. When the Kellogg promotion ended, Bully contracted directly with Peyo to continue production of the figures, a deal that stayed in place until 1977.

By 1980, Schleich obtained the sole rights to the property in Europe, and molds from all the companies became their property. Since then, Schtroumpfs have been in near-constant production and hundreds of different varieties have been designed and fabricated, from comics-inspired Schtroumpfs playing the lute to wilder concepts like Schtroumpfs dressed as different signs of the zodiac.

There has also been a wide array of play sets, including Schtroumpf mushroom cottages of different colors and sizes, Gargamel's castle, and a tree stump environment, which is considered to be an extremely rare and valuable collectible.

La Pitufina

LOS PITUFOS

Peyo

Y LOS PITUFOS TIENEN HAMBRE

PLANETA DeAGOSTINI®

...fra CARLSEN if

Smølferne

ASTROSMØLFEN

og

EN SMØLF IKKE SOM DE ANDRE

af Peyo

DE SMURFEN

HET EI EN DE SMURFEN

Peyo
CREATIONS

4

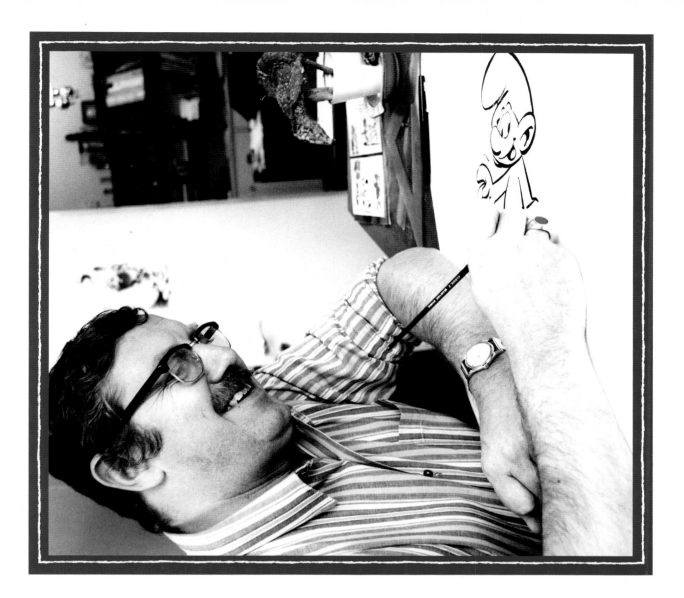

1971. To further broaden the appeal of the Schtroumpfs, Peyo set up a deal with a Dutch magazine to create one-page gag strips that could be run simultaneously in French in the pages of *Spirou*. A volume of these *Histoires de Schtroumpfs* (1972) would later be collected and printed as the eighth book in the growing series.

Other titles from the original set of albums include *L'Oeuf et les Schtroumpfs* (1968), *Les Schtroumpfs et le Cracoucass* (1969), *Schtroumpf Vert et Vert Schtroumpf* (1973), *La Soupe aux Schtroumpfs* (1976), and *Les Schtroumpfs Olympiques* (1976), which was originally serialized to coincide with the 1980 Olympics and was collected with two other stories in 1983.

For a time in the 1970s and early 1980s, the Schtroumpfs comics were forced to take a backseat to the business of the Schtroumpfs themselves, as new venues to tell their stories became available to Peyo through the media contacts he had made in his decades as a cartoonist. While gag strips still appeared in various publications throughout Europe, in the early '70s Peyo decided to take a few steps back in terms of his professional history as an artist and a leap forward in terms of progress as a businessman.

The Schtroumpfs were going to get animated.

OPPOSITE | Since 1963, Schtroumpf comic albums have been translated into twenty-five different languages and have sold upwards of twenty-five million copies worldwide. **RIGHT |** Peyo c. 1971.

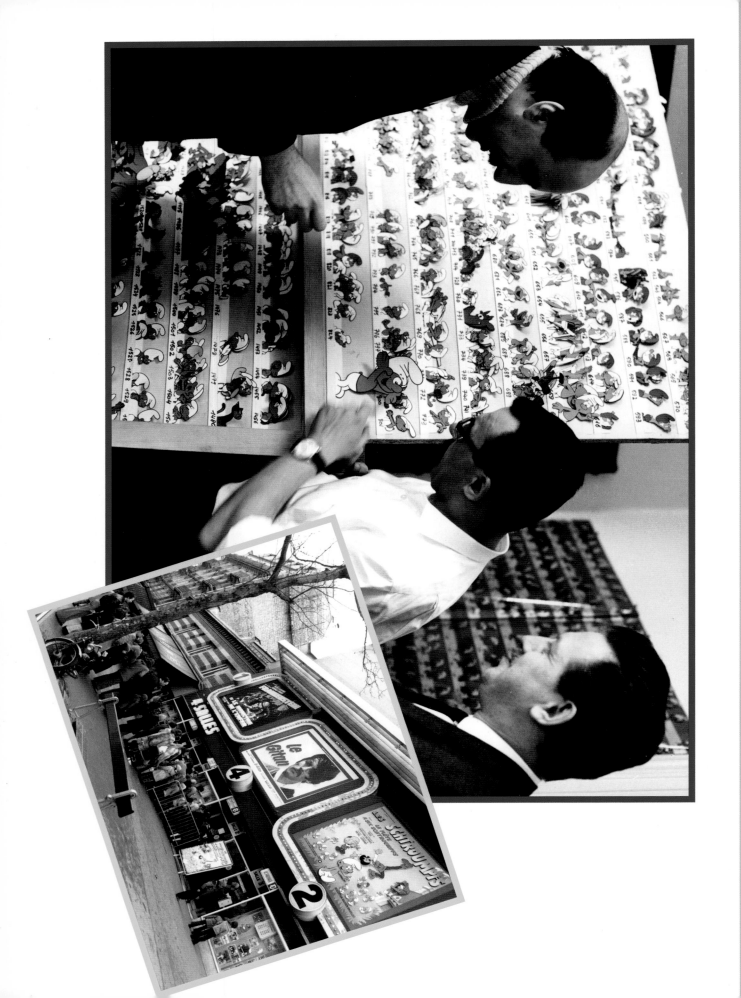

La Flûte à Six Schtroumpfs

During the early 1960s, specific Schtroumpf comics were adapted by TVA Dupuis into animated televised shorts. (These first cartoons were later collected into a compilation film, *Les Aventures des Schtroumpfs*, which has been scarcely seen since its 1965 release.) Though involved in the creation of the shorts during their production, at the time Peyo was more concerned with ensuring that all of the comics coming out of his studio met his rigorous standards of quality storytelling. However, at the beginning of the 1970s, Peyo was offered the opportunity to return to his animation roots and direct a feature-length film about the Schtroumpfs.

Belvision, a Belgian animation company spun-off of *Le Journal Tintin*, was successful in creating animated features out of the comics that had appeared in the pages of their magazine. Recognizing the phenomenon that Peyo had created with the Schtroumpfs, they contacted him about creating a brand-new adventure directly for the screen. Instead, he opted to adapt "La Flûte à Six Trous" (which had since been re-titled *La Flûte à Six Schtroumpfs* when published as an album), and got to work on

OPPOSITE | The television shorts animated by TVA Dupuis were strung together to form *L'Aventure des Schtroumpfs* in 1965; however, the first full-length feature to star the Schtroumpfs, *La Flûte à Six Schtroumpfs*, was released in European cinemas on December 24, 1975. **RIGHT** | Scenes from *La Flûte à Six Schtroumpfs*, directed by Peyo and Eddie Lateste.

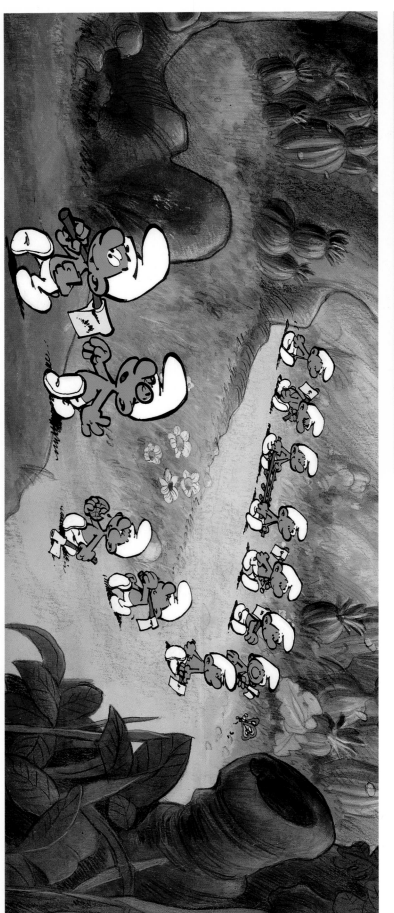

bringing not only the Schtroumpfs to the cinemas but also his beloved original creations, Johan and Pirlouit.

Together Peyo, Delporte, and teams of artists at both Peyo's studio and Belvision worked on making the project in the vein of the musical masterpieces that had come from the Disney studio. The story was already musical in nature thanks to the presence of the magic flute. A team of songwriters, including Oscar-winning composer Michel Legrand, were brought on to craft songs that would fully realize the world of the Schtroumpfs and start to build the characters' musical legacy.

Peyo

La flûte à six SCHTROUMPFS

One song in particular was created to introduce the individual Schtroumpfs that had begun to appear in the over a decade-and-a-half's worth of stories that had appeared in *Spirou* and the collection of Schtroumpf comic albums. Another was created to help Pirlouit understand and eventually speak the Schtroumpf language in proper Schtroumpf, a moment played for humor so well in both the comic and the film.

The original voice cast was filled out by noted French actors and comedians, including Michel Modo (star of the then-popular *Le Gendarme de St. Tropez* film series), and a young Michel Elias, who would later become one of the leading voice-over artists in Europe (providing the French-speaking voices for iconic characters such as Kermit the Frog and Pumbaa from *The Lion King*).

The film was released in Belgium, France, and Holland on Christmas Eve, 1975, and was a success despite receiving criticism for choppy animation. The story and the music were rightfully praised and credited with making the movie somewhat of an instant classic that established the Schtroumpfs as multimedia stars in their native country and surrounding areas.

OPPOSITE | Cels from *La Flûte à Six Schtroumpfs* presented on exquisite backgrounds hand-painted by Studio Peyo artist Matagne; characters drawn by Marc Wasterlain. **RIGHT |** Title page from and (INSERT) a poster for the musical adventure.

GLOBAL VILLAGE

WHILE "LES SCHTROUMPFS" were a national treasure in Belgium, it would take the contributions of a Dutch singer, a British petroleum company, an American television executive, and thousands of international companies to make the Smurfs a worldwide phenomenon.

By the end of the 1980s, millions of children would be calling them various names, from "*Los Pitufos*" (in Spanish); to "*Hupikék Törpikék*" (in Hungarian); to "*Die Schlümpfe*" (in German); to "*Il Puffi*" (in Italian); but it would be the Dutch translation, "*De Smurfen*," that would help identify them for English speakers.

The *Smurfs* would take the world by storm.

Song of the Smurfs

In 1977, to promote the European release of the film *La Flûte à Six Schtroumpfs*, Dupuis, through its licensing arm—La Société d'Edition, de Presse et de Publicité (S.E.P.P.)—reached out to children's entertainer Vader Abraham (Father Abraham, to English speakers) to record a song for the Dutch market.

"The Smurf Song" became an instant hit, quickly selling out of its initial pressing, and a full-length album was commissioned. The record was translated into numerous languages and sold throughout Europe where it went gold, selling over five-hundred thousand copies. It spawned chart-topping singles in sixteen countries. The English translation of "The Smurf Song"

LaLaLaLaLaLa

was the United Kingdom's sixth best-selling record of 1978, preparing that country for one of the most popular marketing campaigns in Smurf history.

That same year, S.E.P.P. contracted with National Benzole (later known as British Petroleum) to launch the "Service with a Smurf" program, which gave buyers a free Smurf PVC figurine with the purchase of gasoline at participating National service stations. According to BBC News, the "promotion quickly turned the two-inch-high pixies into the hottest currency in school playgrounds," securing the Smurfs a strong foothold in the English-speaking market.

S.E.P.P. was determined to use the popularity of the British campaign to cross over into the American marketplace; however, they had difficulties in finding a company that would support foreign characters depicted in plastic. Most distributors wanted to place their own label on recognizable stuffed dolls.

In 1979, Wallace Berrie & Co. acquired the North American licensing rights to the Smurfs and began to import their own versions of the PVC figures using preexisting molds from Dupuis, Bully, and Schleich. While most PVC toys sold for roughly twenty-five cents

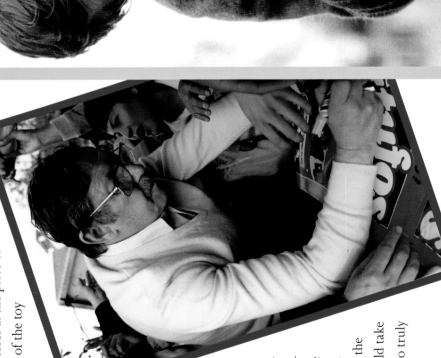

in the late 1970s, Wallace Berrie took the risk of placing the Smurfs in American stores at the price of $1.50, which, to the surprise of the toy industry, didn't deter shoppers from snapping up the little guys (and girl). The company reinvested the revenue into creating more products, including Smurfs plush dolls, which became highly sought-after cuddly collectibles in the United States.

As the toys grew in popularity, the comics were translated and brought over to the United States, but full-blown Smurf-mania had yet to grab the country or the world. It would take a well-placed stuffed Smurf to truly launch that craze . . . .

RIGHT | An international superstar thanks to the success of the "The Smurf Song" and the toys, Peyo signs autographs for Spanish fans (CENTER), and takes a spin with one of his blue buddies c. late 1970s (RIGHT).

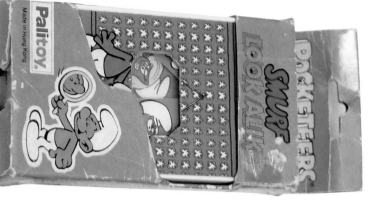

Saturday Morning Superstars

The "Golden Age of Saturday Morning Cartoons" was a period from 1966 to 1990 when all three American television networks (yes, there were only three: ABC, CBS, and NBC) made a conscious decision to devote blocks of their weekend morning programming exclusively to animated programming intended for children.

Early stars of this period were superheroes like Birdman and fictional teenaged rock bands like The Archies, but as time went on, live-action kids' shows and other family-friendly programming began to take over the airwaves, the ratings started to dip, and the future of Saturday morning cartoons as an institution began to seem uncertain.

The late 1970s were an especially bleak time for animated cartoons. Network programmers and animation studios had fallen into a pattern of reusing popular formulas—assembling groups of teenaged crime solvers around a unique mascot character in the *Scooby-Doo* vein, for example. Some just took characters from their most popular shows and paired them together, making them "perform" or "compete" much like their live-action

LEFT | From left to right: A Smurf matching card game from 1975, and a checklist of available Smurf products offered in the U.S. by Wallace-Berrie, so consumers could keep track of their collections. **OPPOSITE** | Peyo in his studio c. 1982.

sitcom and soap-opera counterparts were doing on primetime shows like Battle of the Network Stars.

By 1979, Fred Silverman—a television executive instrumental in ushering in the golden age by helping to develop shows like Space Ghost and Scooby-Doo, Where Are You?—had become the President and CEO of NBC. While on a network trip to Aspen, Colorado, he bought his daughter, Melissa, a plush Smurf doll from a local toy shop. Upon his return, Silverman contacted Joseph Barbera, cofounder of Hanna-Barbera Productions, and charged him with acquiring the rights to the Smurfs, guaranteeing the studio an on-air commitment if they could produce an animated cartoon series around the property.

Barbera did as he was told, and thus began a two-year trip to the television screen that took the Smurfs on some strange twists and turns, veering far from Peyo's 1958 creation before coming back to a familiar form. Among the ideas pitched during the contract and development process: assigning each Smurf a different color (a pink Smurfette!); designing some to resemble famous American film actors and characters (Jokey as Harpo Marx, anyone?); and changing the "Black Smurfs,"

OPPOSITE | Peyo and The Smurfs animation team in front of the Hanna-Barbera studio c. 1982. Directly behind Peyo are (from left to right): Executive Producer Joseph Barbera, producer Gerard Baldwin, Executive Producer William Hanna, and Freddy Monnickendam, head of S.E.P.P. International S.A. **RIGHT** | Original storyboards for the season-three episode "All Creatures Great and Smurf."

LEFT | Before they reached American audiences, "Les Schtroumpfs noirs" were changed to "Purple Smurfs" by Hanna-Barbera. Although it was the first Smurfs comic, the story didn't see publication in English until 2010, when a similar change was made by the American comics publishers Papercutz. (ABOVE) The original Hanna-Barbera model cel depicting the color change of the villainous Bzz Fly.

which were then made purple by the Bzz Fly (to avoid offending African-American audiences).

However, Peyo's contract with NBC, Hanna-Barbera, and S.E.P.P. stipulated that he had veto power over any changes made to his creations. Throughout the process, he and Yvan Delporte, who often served as Peyo's intermediary, stuck to their concepts and saw to it that the property they had created and fostered for more than two decades maintained the integrity and spirit with which the Smurfs were imbued in their original comics.

The result of this creative back-and-forth was a show that would revitalize Saturday mornings. The undeniable cuteness of the characters, their language, and their world would attract a younger demographic, while bringing a long-missing element of magical fantasy to children's entertainment, which appealed to older viewers tired of the same old cartoons.

On September 12, 1981, The Smurfs debuted on NBC and captured 42 percent of the audience that Saturday morning, making it the most highly rated children's program in more than eight years and the highest rated

RIGHT | (TOP) Peyo and his son, Thierry Culliford, at Studio Cartoon Creations c. 1988. (BOTTOM) Yvan Delporte (on the left) and Peyo met in 1955 and their creative partnership lasted until Peyo's death in 1992. Fluent in English, Delporte often served as Peyo's representative when dealing with Hanna-Barbera during the production of *The Smurfs* animated cartoon.

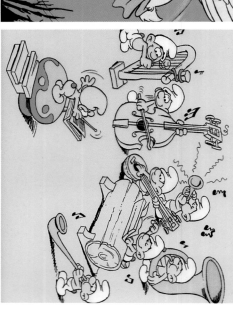

program on NBC in roughly two decades. In terms of viewing percentage, The Smurfs even outpaced a number of successful prime-time shows, including the top-rated drama, Dallas, which claimed anywhere between 30 to 38 percent of total viewers in its time slot.

What made the success of the show especially unique was that it was presented in an hour-long block, in contrast to the typical half-hour duration of most Saturday morning cartoons. This was a scheduling choice fought for by Joe Barbera, not only because of the financial implications for his company—an hour provided twice as much revenue for Hanna-Barbera Productions and their producing partners, S.E.P.P. International—but also, as Barbera believed, because it allowed for the show to fully capture the imagination of the viewing public.

In his 1994 autobiography My Life in 'toons, Barbera wrote: "The show was an excursion into fantasy. Effective fantasy requires you to create and populate an entire world and that takes time. The great fantasy writers wrote long novels. Just think of J.R.R. Tolkien's Lord of the Rings and so on. Letting The Smurfs have an hour to do their thing gave the show enough time to create a convincing realm of fantasy."

LEFT | (TOP) Animation cel featuring Papa Smurf and his sunlit bedroom. This room background would be reused in many episodes during the show's run. (BOTTOM) A promotional shot from an episode, and a variation on a popular image from the book Smurfony in C. **OPPOSITE |** A promotional photograph of a young June Foray c. 1952.

June Foray:
First Lady of Cartoon Voices

While *The Smurfs* voice cast was filled with seasoned and familiar voices, such as Don Messick as Papa (he also voiced Scooby-Doo and Astro Jetson), Frank Welker (Megatron from *The Transformers* cartoon) as Hefty, and Michael Bell (GI *Joe*'s Duke) as Handy, perhaps one of the most memorable performances from the series was June Foray's turn as Jokey Smurf, the village prankster.

While she was originally up for the part of Smurfette (which went to Lucille Bliss, *Crusader Rabbit*), Foray was encouraged by director Gordon Hunt to try out for other characters. After noticing an interesting word, written in a line for another Smurf—"Hyuck!"—she played with it, and Jokey's distinctive laugh was born.

Besides Jokey, Foray's most famous creations are perhaps Rocket J. Squirrel, Bullwinkle's high-flying companion from Jay Ward's *The Rocky and Bullwinkle Show*; and Granny, Tweety and Sylvester's owner in the *Looney Tunes* shorts (a part she has played on and off since 1955). Her voice has also been heard as Warner Bros. character Witch Hazel; Cindy Lou Who in *How the Grinch Stole Christmas*

(1966); and both Mattel's real-life Chatty Cathy doll and her fictional *Twilight Zone* counterpart, the murderous Talky Tina.

As the producers and writers added newer characters in later seasons of *The Smurfs*, Foray was encouraged to audition for more roles, one of which was Mother Nature. Rightly assuming that other actors would imitate her own wizened, matronly Granny voice in their auditions, Foray chose to play the role "ditzy" on her tape and won the part in an anonymous casting process—because Joe Barbera liked the fact that she "wasn't doing June Foray!"

In addition to her performances, Foray has contributed to the recognition of voice-acting as a Governor of both the Academy of Motion Pictures Arts and Sciences, and the National Academy of Recording Arts and Sciences, and she has long been a member and supporter of the International Animated Film Society (ASIFA). In 1995, ASIFA-Hollywood established the June Foray Award for individuals who have made a significant and benevolent or charitable impact on the art and industry of animation.

During its history-making nine-year original run on Saturday mornings—from September 1981 to December 1989—The Smurfs would at one point expand to a ninety-minute format and would generate 272 episodes that featured a grand total of 421 different short stories. NBC also aired seven holiday specials including The Smurfs Springtime Special (1982), My Smurfy Valentine (1983), and 'Tis the Season to Be Smurfy (1987).

Animation writer and producer Alan Burnett (who in the early 1990s would help to create Batman: The Animated Series) worked on The Smurfs from 1982 to 1987, serving as one of the series' story editors in the 1986 and 1987 seasons. He remembers the process of creating the weekly program as "the hardest, most time consuming show I've ever worked on. Peyo, the creator, had his vision of the characters, which we tried to adhere to," he recalls. "And then you had network demands (of internal standards and practices) . . . and a schedule that was as unforgiving as a high-speed conveyor belt . . . and ninety minutes to fill each week."

While many of the original comics were adapted for the first season of the television show, including "La Schtroumpfs

LEFT | Since her first appearance in "La Schtroumpfette," the other Smurfs' affection for Smurfette has served as a plot device to drive conflict and competition, as depicted in these promotional illustrations.

et le Cracoucass" ("The Smurfs and the Howlibird"), and "Le Schtroumpfissime" ("King Smurf"), Hanna-Barbera quickly reached a point where new characters had to be introduced and original stories had to be created just for the series.

A natural addition to the cast was Johan. He and Pirlouit (now called Peewit) started making cameos in second-season episodes of The Smurfs before having episodes devoted to them that were adapted from the original Johan et Pirlouit comics. Enough Johan and Peewit cartoons were produced by Hanna-Barbera that the material was repackaged and sold as a spin-off in foreign markets.

"I was story editor for two years, and about a third of the way through each season you wondered if you'd ever make it to the end," says Burnett. "We were so desperate for new Smurfs, we would actually go through the Yellow Pages to come up with ideas."

While Burnett estimates that roughly half of the material generated by Hanna-Barbera's writers never moved beyond Peyo and Delporte's offices, a number of characters created for use in the animated series did pass muster, and eventually crossed over into the Peyo

RIGHT | Selected character model sheets c. 1989.

comics albums. Baby Smurf and the Smurflings, who made their first appearances in 1983 and 1985, respectively, were two such creations.

Some characters were given the initial approval of Peyo's studio for use in the cartoon show but in limited roles that ensured their popularity wouldn't overshadow that of the Smurfs themselves. In the case of the Pixies in particular, Delporte feared that Hanna-Barbera would use The Smurfs to launch spin-off cartoon shows—re-creating, in a way, the situation that birthed the Smurfs phenomenon from the pages of Johan et Pirlouit.

In 1983, one very special character was introduced to the Smurf village: Laconia, a mute wood elf who teaches the Smurfs sign language. Originally aired on November 19, 1983, "Smurfing in Sign Language" was the first cartoon on American television to use sign language as a form of communication, and earned praise for providing Laconia as a role model for deaf children. It was co-written by Patsy Cameron, who had served as the sign language interpreter for President Jimmy Carter's 1977 inaugural address and for addresses made by Pope John Paul II in Philadelphia and Washington, DC.

In a December 1983 press release for the episode,

LEFT | The Smurflings made their first appearance in the premiere episode of Season Five in 1985. Nearly three years later, the two-part story was adapted into a comic album published in Europe by Dupuis.

Cameron, then a story editor (and the first woman to hold that title in Hanna-Barbera's history), stated that: "One of the symbols we will demonstrate in this episode includes the sign of the cat, so the Smurfs can warn each other about Azrael without the cat hearing them. Another important one is the symbol for 'I Love You,' which is the thought expressed in every Smurfs episode we write."

Her contributions as writer helped the show to win its second Daytime Emmy for Outstanding Children's Entertainment Series in 1984 (its prior win in that category was in the previous year) and The Smurfs would be nominated for a total of five more Emmys in the category of Outstanding Animated Series. In 1987, the show and writers Burnett and John Loy would also win a Humanitas Prize for "writers whose work explores the human condition in a nuanced, meaningful way."

By season nine, when over one hundred hours of The Smurfs cartoons had been created, the team had run out of comics to adapt and professions to pluck from the phone book—whereupon the writers and producers sent the Smurfs journeying through time to encounter versions of characters such as Gargamel, Hogatha, and

RIGHT | In this piece of artwork from Hanna-Barbera, Laconia the mute wood elf shows Smurfette the sign for butterfly.

Paul Winchell: Evil Wizard or Medical Hero? Both!

Paul Winchell (1922–2005) may have voiced the villainous Gargamel, but the actor was also a medical hero, having contributed to the design of the first artificial heart in collaboration with Dr. Henry Heimlich (of Heimlich Maneuver fame).

Before becoming known as a children's entertainer and ventriloquist thanks to numerous appearances on television shows throughout the 1950s and 1960s, and his own program *Winchell-Mahoney Time* (1965–1968), Winchell studied pre-med at Columbia University. A noted inventor, Winchell also held patents for dozens of other inventions, including a disposable razor, a plasma defroster, a flameless lighter, and battery-heated gloves. In the 1980s, he focused his attention on ending world hunger by developing a method of farming freshwater fish in sub-Saharan Africa.

Despite all of these accomplishments, Winchell is best known for entertaining generations of children as a voice actor whose distinctive roles included Tigger from *Winnie the Pooh*, Dick Dastardly from *The Perils of Penelope Pitstop*, and, of course, the Smurfs' chief menace!

CARTOON
CREATION s.a.
BRUSSELS
14 TH MAY
6.00 PM

FROM : PEYO
JAN M^c CURDY
TO

PLEASE FIND HEREAFTER "SCRUPLE":
THE NEW MODEL- SHEET OF CORRECTED PREMISES
YOU WILL RECEIVE

EARLY NEXT WEEK.

LOVE,
Peyo

NUMBER OF PAGES : 4 (THIS ONE INCLUDE

Scruple specific to a certain historic place. To many, it marked the point when *The Smurfs* "jumped the shark"; regardless, it would be the *The Smurfs*' last season.

Hanna-Barbera would animate the characters only one other time, for *Cartoon All-Stars to the Rescue*, a prime-time special that ham-handedly delivered an antidrug message to kids via their favorite cartoon characters. As they were reluctant to combine a drug message with the Smurfs out of concern that very young audiences would not understand, Peyo and company limited the Smurfs' use to the opening sequence.

By 1990, *The Smurfs* had been cancelled by NBC, which by this point was getting rid of its animated Saturday morning lineup to allow for more news programming and the creation of a weekend edition of their hit *Today Show*. The "Golden Age of Saturday Morning," was indeed over, but there's no doubt the Smurfs had been key players in its existence.

Smurfs Alive!

The Smurfs animated series was responsible not only for popularizing the characters in America, but also for bringing them into millions of homes in over

OPPOSITE | Paul Winchell c. 1953 with dummies Jerry Mahoney and Knucklehead Smiff. **RIGHT** | Peyo and his studio were very involved in the creation and design of new characters for the animated series, such as Scruple, who first appeared in season six.

forty-seven countries including Italy, Spain, Mexico, Brazil, and Thailand.

In addition, the cartoons opened the door to numerous licensing opportunities that soon had the Smurfs appearing on thousands of products sold the world over, from bedsheets to breakfast cereals. In 1982 alone, Smurfs merchandise was estimated as bringing in $600 million in retail sales.

Equal efforts were made not just to bring the blue imps into households, but to bring families into the world of the Smurfs.

In 1984, Taft Entertainment, which at the time owned Hanna-Barbera, began to open Smurf-themed attractions at theme parks it ran through the Kings Entertainment Corporation. Smurf villages, water rides, and roller coasters became popular amusements at their Kings Island (Ohio), Kings Dominion (Virginia), Carowinds (North Carolina), and Great America (California) locations. The company even opened a Smurf Forest at Canada's Wonderland, near Toronto.

The Smurfs also toured stadiums as a part of the popular Ice Capades figure skating show. The costumes

LEFT | From top: A souvenir banner from the Ice Capades' "Smurfs Alive" presentation, and a variety of Smurfs memorabilia from 1959 to the present.

originally used in their 1982 *Smurfs Alive!* program were reused for other presentations, and distributed to their Ice Capades Chalets: stationary rinks located throughout America that offered regular entertainment and training programs for young skaters.

This kind of promotional blitz became the industry standard when dealing with children's entertainment properties during the 1980s. The practice drew the attention of organizations of concerned adults who argued that children couldn't tell the difference between an episode of *The Smurfs* and an ad featuring them. Yet they couldn't argue that it was the heart of the characters that drew the world's children, and legions of "grownups," to everything Smurfy. Since the characters went global, over two-thousand companies have been responsible for producing Smurfs memorabilia.

Stephen Parkes, a thirty-plus-year collector and holder of the 2011 Guinness World Record for most Smurfs owned, sums up the characters' cross-market, cross-generational allure: "I think it's their ideals, the fact that they are so helpful, have no vices, and appeal to a wide audience from kids right up to adults."

RIGHT | Peyo finds himself waist high in only a sampling of the Smurfs merchandise available in the early 1980s.

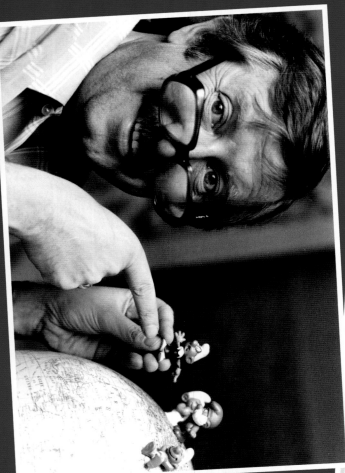

Bonsoir, Papa

On Christmas Eve 1992, Pierre "Peyo" Culliford died of a heart attack. The Smurfs had lost their true Papa. And although their television show—the medium through which millions had come to know them—had ended, the Smurfs continued to live on through the 1990s, thanks in large part to the efforts of the Culliford family.

International Merchandising, Promotion & Services (I.M.P.S), a company founded in 1984 by Peyo's daughter Véronique, continued to license the property throughout the world. While American companies were shutting down their Smurf theme park attractions, I.M.P.S. was arranging for Big Bang Schtroumpf to open in Lorraine, France. Even though the property changed hands a number of times since opening its doors in 1989, the park remained Smurf-themed until 2003.

The Smurfs also continued to appear in new comics produced by Peyo's studio and distributed by Le Lombard in Europe. Although his son Thierry had long ago assumed control of the studio (calling it Cartoon Creations) and other artists had been drawing the characters for years, Peyo's monograph remained on all new artwork that featured the Smurfs, Johan, or Benoît Brisefer—the mark of a proud papa.

LEFT | By 1982 Peyo had become the head of a global media empire. Toward the end of his life he returned to creating new comics, starting with the album *L'Aéroschtroumpf* in 1989.

OPPOSITE | The Smurfs' "Papa" at his desk in 1983.

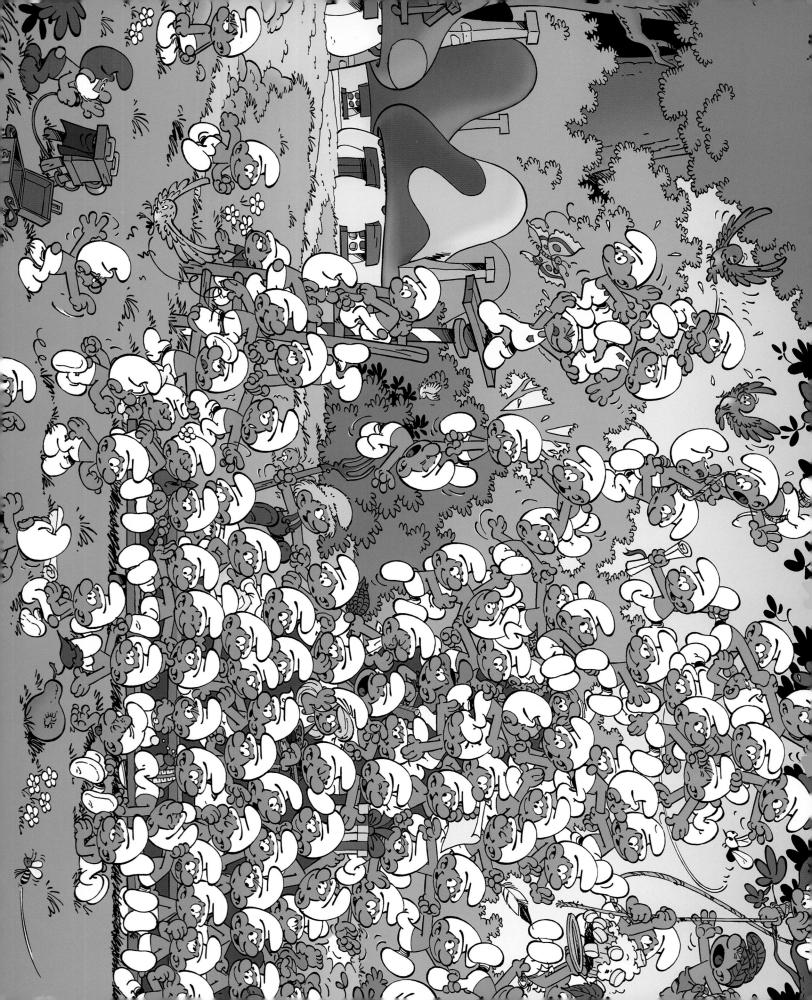

WHO THE SMURF?!

AS WE'VE TAKEN a look at how and why they became so beloved by so many people, it's high time we took a look at whom we're smurfing about, when we smurf about the Smurfs.

Smurf

There is a "basic" Smurf who inhabits the Smurf Village. In fact, in the early adventures there were roughly ninety-nine of them. Their individual personalities wouldn't be developed or revealed until the comics caught on. Later, some were even given different wardrobe pieces or physical markers to truly differentiate them from the pack and make them easily identifiable to readers, viewers, and the countless inter-national artists who would have to depict the specific characters in various media despite knowing them by different names or through different attributes.

But the "basic" Smurf is the model on which all others are fashioned and requires some examination for definition and identification purposes. Here's some elementary Smurfology:

HEIGHT: The Smurfs are "three apples high." What non-French-speaking fans might not understand is that this is a direct translation of the idiom "haut comme trois pommes," a catchy turn of phrase meaning that something is really small. An English equivalent would be "knee-high to a grasshopper." (Some legitimize the "three apple" concept by saying that Smurfs are roughly

BASIC SMURFS

WRONG

THERE ARE SUBTLE TURNS IN THE
CURVE OF THE SMURF HAT

BUT DO NOT LET THEM
BECOME POINTS

THE SMURFS NEW MODELS

STANDARD COMPARATIVE SIZE

APR 27 1989

© HANNA-BARBERA PRODUCTIONS INC. FROM PEYO

0128-0900

BABY SMURF

SMURFS

2

The "Land of the Smurfs" is located far, far, far from here, and very rare are the human beings who have ever gone there.

the height of three European crabapples—generally smaller than their American cousins and therefore, perhaps, just about right.)

GENDER: The Smurfs are all male. There is no naturally occurring female of the Smurfs species, although some have been created through the use of magic. Smurfs do not reproduce, per se, but rather baby Smurfs are delivered via stork on the rare occurrence of a magical Blue Moon.

COLOR: Blue. Duh!?!

CLOTHING: The basic Smurf wears a white bonnet based on the Phrygian caps worn by traditional pixies from Celtic myths. The hat is also a French symbol of liberation and freedom. Smurfs are bald underneath and usually otherwise hairless. They complete their ensemble with a pair of matching white pants that have a hole cut out to accommodate their tail. Only Papa Smurf deviates greatly from this model, as he wears a red outfit indicating his status, and a bushy white beard showing his age.

HABITAT: Located in the Cursed Land (le Pays maudit), the Smurf Village is an enclave of mushrooms

OPPOSITE | These size-comparison charts were taken from a "model pack" given to Hanna-Barbera animators to ensure that the Smurfs retained a uniform appearance from drawing to drawing. **RIGHT** | The first "aerial" drawing of the Smurf Village, originally done for the 1963 album *Les Schtroumpfs Noirs*; English translation from the 2010 Papercutz graphic novel *The Purple Smurfs*.

nestled between the mountains and the Smurf River. Very well hidden in the Cursed Land Forest, the village is almost never found by human explorers unless they're transported there mystically or are physically led there by a Smurf. (Gargamel does stumble upon it once, in "La Soupe aux Schtroumpfs.")

LANGUAGE: The Smurfs speak Smurf, a curious tongue that requires more of a conscious understanding of what one is discussing than an expansive vocabulary. On the surface, it would seem that any word, be it noun or verb, can simply be replaced by the word "smurf"; however, non-native speakers often find their meaning lost when they use "smurf" arbitrarily, as they also lose context. The language even has regional dialects, depending on what part of the Smurf Village one is from. The comic "Schtroumpf vert et vert Schtroumpf" (1972) depicts a conflict between Smurfs from the north side of the village and those from the south side over the proper use of "smurf." The issue is never truly resolved, leaving the fate of the language to the mouths and ears of the speakers.

DIET: The main staple of the Smurfs' diet and the base of many of Papa Smurf's formulas is "salsepareille," a mystical plant that grows wild just outside

LEFT | Peewit gets his first lesson in "smurfing Smurf" in this scene from *The Smurfs and the Magic Flute.* **IN POUCH |** This promotional poster was originally created by Peyo's studio for *Schtroumpf!* magazine c. early 1990s.

Someone broke my guitar! And I was smurfing a serenade to Smurfette!

Ha! Ha! Well done!

And I hate you!

I despise you!

Me, I hate Smurfs who like Smurfette!

Hey, Brainy! You, go smurf me some...

Not now Papa Smurf! Later!

Oh! Hefty Smurf, Shmefty Smurf! He looks strong, but deep down, he's not as strong as all that!

And what had to happen, happened. Discord, enmity, jealousy—feelings till then unknown to the Smurfs—destroyed the lovely harmony that had heretofore prevailed among them.

of the Smurf Village. Yvan Delporte introduced it to the comics because he found the name magical, and the word seemed so foreign to Peyo that he originally believed his partner made it up. An actual plant native to the Americas, sarsaparilla (*smilax regelii*) is commonly used on the other side of the Atlantic as the basis of soft drinks, namely root beer. As the plant was by no means exotic to Americans, references to sarsaparilla were changed to Smurfberries and Smurfberry bushes when the writers of the cartoon began adapting the comics.

ABOVE | Smurfs demonstrate various uses of the word "smurf" in a panel from *The Smurfette*. **RIGHT** | A Smurf happily chomps on a "sarsaparilla" leaf.

Smurfs of Note:

Now that we understand the basics, and can sound a lot smurfier at dinner parties, scientific symposia, and comic conventions alike, the following is a glossary of some of the key players from the comics and cartoon series that left their tiny footprints on the hearts and minds of countless fans.

Baby

Although the character known simply as Baby Smurf was dropped on account of a clerical error, the Smurfs are eventually allowed to keep him because of the love they show for the new arrival. In the animated series, Baby is depicted as magical and it is alluded to that he may be the next "Papa" Smurf.

Brainy

Called simply "le Schtroumpf à Lunettes" (the Smurf with Glasses) or previously called "le Schtroumpf Moralisateur" (Moralizing Smurf) in the comics, Brainy is one of the few Smurfs who has a history dating back to "Les Schtroumpfs noirs." In both the strip and the animated cartoon show, Brainy is depicted as a know-it-all who often gives condescending speeches to the others. While in the printed stories, he is punished for his haughty demeanor by a whack to the head with a mallet, the cartoon changed that to his being physically tossed out of the village—out of fear that viewers would hit children they didn't like on the head with a hammer.

Clumsy

Whether in the comics or the cartoon show, Clumsy is depicted as a good-hearted, well-meaning Smurf whose intentions are spoiled by his own two feet . . . which he falls over often. As he's somewhat dim-witted, it seems only natural that Clumsy's best friend would be Brainy, the self-professed smartest Smurf in the village.

Cook/Baker & Greedy

A Smurf whose role it is to prepare food for the village and another with an overwhelming compulsion to eat all of it make for quite the comedy team, and an easy gag to play out with very little dialogue—allowing the art to speak for itself. Although created as different characters in the comics, Cook/Baker and Greedy were combined in the animated series, making Greedy a chef who loves his job a bit too much.

Dreamy

First mentioned in the comics, the character of Dreamy was popularized in the animated series where he served as a composite of several Smurfs from the original stories. His daydreams take him to far-off places, inspiring him to embark on his own real adventures. His most famous escapade was his imagined trip to the stars as "The Astrosmurf" (The Smurfs series premiere, adapted from the comic Le Cosmoschtroumpf), which had him encountering the Swoofs (really the other Smurfs in disguise). Future episodes featured him as the captain of his own sailing ship, the S.S. Smurf II.

Grandpa

With what's assumed to be close to one thousand smurfdays (birthdays, to non-smurfers) under his hat, Grandpa Smurf was rightfully called "le Vieux Vieux Schtroumpf" (the Old Old Smurf) when he made his transition from the American cartoons into the French comics. He was Papa Smurf's Papa Smurf, who, in the TV series, left his village to go on a five-hundred-year quest to restore power to the Long Life Stone. In the American cast of the animated series he was played by Jonathan Winters, who would lend his voice to Papa Smurf in the 2011 Smurfs film.

Grouchy

Once an unnamed Smurf, Grouchy took on his chief characteristic and his name when he was bitten by the Bzz Fly in the comic "Les Schtrompfs noirs." Although all of the other Smurfs return to normal when Papa Smurf cures them at the end of that story, later scripts have one character talking about how he "hates" most aspects of everyday life, causing other Smurfs to notice how grouchy he'd become since the whole ordeal. While he generally doesn't like anything, he does have a soft spot in his heart for Baby Smurf and later the Smurflings; and in "L'Oeuf et les Schtroumpfs" ("The Egg and the Smurfs") we learn that his secret heart's desire is to love everything. This back-story was ignored by writers of the animated series, who depicted Grouchy in full sulk during the first episode of the show.

You had a smurfy fall, Grumpy... I'll take care of you!

I don't like falling down and I don't like being taken care of!

I'll smurf a bandage on... you'd better take it easy for a while!

I don't like bandages and I don't like people smurfing me advice.

Right!... Now for your foot!

50

Handy

Handy is the village inventor and resident "Mr. Fix-it." Despite living in the Middle Ages, he did manage to create advanced technology, the walking, talking proof of that being Clockwork Smurf, Handy's wooden robot helper. In the early 1970s, Peyo and company began depicting Handy in a blue apron, then blue overalls, which were adapted to his white outfit made famous by the animated series.

Harmony

Called "le Schtroumpf Musicien" in French, Harmony came by his English name ironically, as the music he plays is always off-key, regardless of the instrument he's playing—though his favorite seems to be the trumpet. He starred in one of the first large-format Smurf comics, "Schtroumpfonie en Ur" (1963), which was adapted as the 1981 cartoon "Smurfony in 'C.'"

Hefty

Though he may look as though he's built like all of the others, Hefty is the strongest Smurf in the Smurf Village. His heart-shaped arm tattoos were given to him during the development of the animated series in order to differentiate him from the other Smurfs, presumably making him seem tougher than the rest. As the Smurf who most resembled an action hero, Hefty was chosen to star in a number of the Smurfs' video games, including The Smurfs' Nightmare, in which he rescues his blue brethren from bad dreams caused by Gargamel.

Jokey

"Le Schtroumpf Farceur" (the Joker Smurf) is a master of practical jokes, though his favorite is the exploding gag gift, as evidenced by his frequent use of it in both the comics and the cartoons. One of the most sought-after Smurf figurines depicts Jokey with his trademark yellow box that opens to reveal a spring-loaded Gargamel head.

Lazy

Although modern medicine would probably diagnose him with narcolepsy, "Lazy" Smurf got his name by sleeping through life . . . literally. Even in his dreams, his thoughts are of sleeping, as seen when he fantasizes about winning a pillow as a medal in "Les Schtroumpfs Olympiques" (1980).

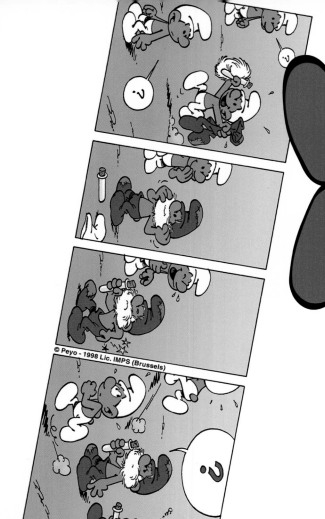

© Peyo - 1998 Lic. IMPS (Brussels)

Papa

Papa Smurf (aka "le Grand Schtroumpf") is the leader of the Smurf Village and a powerful practitioner of magic. The first Smurf to have his own identity, Papa was introduced in the pages of "La Flûte à Six Trous," where he declared himself to be 542 years old (the rest of the Smurfs being only about one hundred or so years old). Though he is generally kind and benevolent, the early Smurfs comics depict him with a mighty temper when he's had enough of anyone's antics.

Nanny

Nanny is the only female Smurf whose existence lacks explanation. All that we know of her past is that she knew Grandpa Smurf over five hundred years ago, before she was abducted by the evil Castle Captor—an enchanted building that appears every five centuries to kidnap unwitting travelers. She never appeared in the comics, and was the last major character to be created for the animated series. In "The Lost Smurf" (1988), Grandpa and a team of Smurfs manage to save Nanny from the castle and return her to the village, where she becomes a matronly figure to everyone, including Papa Smurf.

Smurfette

Created by Gargamel to spy on and help him destroy the Smurf Village, Papa Smurf's magic and Smurfette's own will helped her overcome her origins to become the sweetheart we know her as today. While critics of *The Smurfs* consider the character and some of her storylines to be sexist in nature, those more familiar with Smurfette know that she's not just a damsel in distress but a free-thinking contributor to the welfare of Smurf-kind. Her unique role as the village female (until Sassette came along, that is), allowed her to be the most heavily marketed character in the property. Since her first appearance in 1966, she has appeared on everything from jewelry boxes to cosmetics.

Smurflings

Natural (aka Nat), Slouchy, and Snappy Smurfling were originally the same age as the other Smurfs in the village, before they were "de-aged" approximately fifty years by a magical clock. As Father Time could only find a way to reverse time, the trio found themselves stuck at their newer, younger ages. The Smurflings also found it difficult to adapt to their new lives in the village but discovered a kindred spirit in Smurfette, who, as the only female Smurf, perceived herself as an outsider. After discovering that Smurfette was created by Gargamel, the Smurflings decided to make Smurfette a sister to make her feel better. They stole the wizard's formula and enough clay to make a smaller female. Like Smurfette before her, she was inadvertently made to be destructive, but as she was pint-size only came off as "sassy"—hence she was named Sassette. Of course, Papa managed to turn her good, but they all discovered she was a bit of a tomboy, much to Smurfette's chagrin and the other Smurflings' enjoyment. They had created a sister not only for Smurfette, but for themselves!

Wild

Wild was intended to be delivered at the same time as the other Smurfs in the village, but he was accidently lost in the outlying forest and was subsequently raised by squirrels. He first appeared in the animated cartoon "Smurf on the Wild Side" (1987), the premiere show of season seven. Like Baby and the Smurflings, he would become a series regular and would eventually be adapted into the comics, starring in his own French-language Smurfs album, *Le Schtroumpf Sauvage* (1998).

© Peyo - 2000 Lic. IMPS

Vanity

As his name implies, Vanity (which is directly translated from "le Schtroumpf Coquet") is concerned almost exclusively with his appearance. Although he lacked the trademark flower in his cap for his first appearance in "Le Schtroumpfissme" (1964), his external character traits were standardized by "La Schtroumpfette" (1966). The Smurfs' official site describes Vanity as: "Delicate and sensitive . . . . he spends his time talking fabrics with Smurfette and keeping his complexion fresh."

Humans, Animals & Others:

Gargamel is an evil human alchemist, who, with Azrael, first appeared in the 1959 comic "Le Voleur des Schtroumpfs" ("The Smurfnapper"). Though his motives for capturing the Smurfs vacillate between eating them and turning them into gold, his hatred for them is apparent in every story in which he appears. Gargamel was named after one of the creatures in Rabelais' 1532 novel *Gargantua*, and is played in three dimensions by Emmy Award-winning actor Hank Azaria (*The Simpsons*) in Sony's live-action/CGI hybrid Smurfs movie.

Azrael is Gargamel's mangy, flea-bitten sidekick, who often serves as the wizard's scapegoat when their schemes to capture the Smurfs go awry—as they always do. Fans of the animated cartoon often debated Azrael's gender, as the cat is always referred to as an "it"; however, those who have read the comic know that he is definitely a male.

Lord Balthazar is an evil sorcerer and Gargamel's godfather. His magic is more powerful and his plans are

much more deadly than those of his former apprentice. He has a niece named **Denisa**, who befriends Sassette in season eight of the animated series.

Bigmouth ("Grossbouf" in French) is an overgrown ogre with a large appetite. More of a nuisance than a villain, Bigmouth has appeared both in the animated series and the comics and is friendly not only with Gargamel but also with the Smurfs, once they come to understand him.

Hogatha, a dumpy, snorting witch who tries in vain to cover her baldness with an ill-fitting wig, was created for the animated series in an effort to add more villains to the cast. She was as much of an annoyance to Gargamel, whom she called "Garglesmell," as to the Smurfs themselves. Peyo and Delporte found the character distasteful, making them reluctant to use her in their comics.

Homnibus was a human enchanter from the *Johan et Pirlouit* comic series. As he was the kingdom's wizard, Johan and Peewit often turned to him for answers when their adventures had a mystical or magical bent. He often appeared in the animated series, especially the "Adventures of Johan and Peewit" segments, which started airing in the second season.

RIGHT | (CLOCKWISE FROM TOP) Characteristic poses for Hogatha, Bigmouth, and Lord Balthazar.

Johan is depicted as a squire and then a knight in service to the King. The character comes from a rich tradition of French literature depicting noble medieval heroes, and Peyo's love of adventure films like 1939's *The Adventures of Robin Hood.*

The King is the monarch of Johan's kingdom, which includes the Cursed Land. In the animated series he has a young relative named **Gerard** whom the Smurfs help install as the ruler of a neighboring kingdom.

Feathers is a friend of the Smurfs and the stork responsible for transporting them around.

Laconia is a mute wood elf whom Papa Smurf called upon when he needed help dealing with aural magic. By the airing of the 1983 special "Smurfily Ever After," she had married her boyfriend Woody, another elf.

Mother Nature is the personification of the natural world and is responsible for making sure that the seasons run smoothly. Her brother, Harold, is the Man in the Moon.

Peewit (aka Pirlouit) is the heroic Johan's comic sidekick and the self-appointed court entertainer—despite the King's protestations about his lousy singing and horrible musicianship. His pet goat, Biquette, is

LEFT | (CLOCKWISE FROM TOP LEFT) Scruple, Peewit, and the amiable Puppy.

named and modeled after the favorite childhood pet of Peyo's wife, Nine.

Puppy, a gift of Hommibus, arrived at the village bearing a locket only Baby could open, making Baby Puppy's true master. Yvan Delporte remembered the character as being the product of Hanna-Barbera's in-house formula to put a dog in all of their cartoons to broaden a show's appeal. However, when show writers created a blue Smurf-size pet for Baby, Studio Peyo objected and helped remodel Puppy into a magical creature in the shape of a "real" dog.

Scruple is Gargamel's young nephew and apprentice. He was introduced to the animated series in the 1986–1987 season, becoming one of The Smurfs' chief baddies. Like Hogatha before him, Scruple became more of a foil for Gargamel than the Smurfs. When he showed any interest in his uncle's hare-brained schemes, it was often to point out the obvious flaws or to poke holes in the wizard's theories.

Smoogle is Nanny Smurf's pink pet marsupial that she befriended during her time in Castle Captor. Like Nanny, Smoogle was rescued from the castle and goes on to live with the Smurfs in their village.

RIGHT | A colorful array of Smurf stickers.

21ST SMURFERY

Collectors' Market

WHILE THEY MAINTAINED their profile in their native Europe, and especially in French-speaking countries where new comic albums were released regularly, for the most part, the Smurfs were viewed as a piece of '80s nostalgia. This was definitely the case in America, where the cultural landscape had begun to produce new fads and marketing booms before the old ones even had a chance to bust.

As the animated heyday of the Smurfs drifted further into memory with the passing decades, fans and critics wondered: Could tiny gnomes that traveled via storks and snail carriages find their way in the twenty-first-century world of internet super highways? Absosmurfly.

While still active in Belgium and France, especially in the pages of Cartoon Creations' *Schtroumpf* magazine, which featured new Smurfs comics, American and British Smurf fans found the 1990s a little less smurfy. With no new cartoons and translations of the comics not readily available, the stream of Smurf merchandise, seemingly endless only a few short years before, had all but dried up on the shores of the United States and the United Kingdom in the 1990s.

This drove collectors to examine their preexisting wares a little more closely and share what they had with the world. The internet, still in its infancy, provided just the right avenue for a global community to

develop. Internet fan sites and online collectors' clubs began to populate the web.

"Until the internet I genuinely thought that I was the only person who collected Smurfs . . . well, certainly one of the very few who still collected them!" recalls Alan Mechem, a lifelong Smurf collector and host of the BBC's *Retrospectacular*, a program about pop culture collectibles. "Belgium certainly has the edge nowadays [in terms of new material being available]. It's amazing going there and seeing the Smurfs so popular . . . in every toy shop and even painted on walls."

As a result of the cultural exchange among collectors, people became aware of promotions that were happening across the globe and of holes they didn't realize were in their collections. "I think the most positive experience is meeting other Smurf collectors," says collector Stephen Parkes, who achieved his own place of note in the global Smurf Village in the pages of the *Guinness Book of World Records*. He admits that it was only through the help of the Internet community that he was able to achieve his record-holding collection of over 1,061 Smurfs and counting (the count was over 1,200 as of October 2010). "They are true to the nature of the

PREVIOUS | A diorama featuring PVC figurines made available by Schleich from the 1970s to the present.

LEFT | (CLOCKWISE FROM TOP) A complete "mini-pixi" village (among the hardest-to-find collectibles), a Smurf Collectors Club card, and an assortment of European board games.

Smurfs and are always really friendly and willing to help. Just like the Smurfs!"

However, both Mechem and Parkes are quick to point out that there are a few "Gargamels" out there on the internet, some of whom—like the villain himself—have tried to pass off their own creations as original Smurfs to improperly and illegally meet the demand for rare collectibles with bogus supply. To some, even collecting "fakes" has become a part of the hobby itself, and a market has sprung up around them, turning quite a profit for unscrupulous dealers and uninformed traders on internet auction sites.

Mechem warns: "Stay away from weirdos and people to whom collecting is just a 'who has more' game . . . and stick to your morals. It's only worth the price you pay!"

The Red (and Blue) Scare

When a property reaches the heights of success that the Smurfs hit in the 1980s, it's bound to have some detractors ready to tear it down and conspiracy theorists looking for evil messages that simply are not there.

While the Smurfs comics had no overarching social or political agenda, some stories, such as "Schtroumpf

RIGHT | Just a few of Schleich's "Super Smurf" figurines, which incorporated larger accessories into their design such as bed sets, automobiles, and sport paraphernalia.

He Who Smurfs Last . . .

During the 1990s and early 2000s, the first generation of international Smurf fans was coming into its own and started creating books, movies, and television shows, and the effect of The Smurfs was felt in the flexing of creative muscles. It is said that the true test of any intellectual property or cultural landmark is the ability to be referenced in non-related media and to not only be the subject of parody, but also withstand it. The Smurfs certainly did that.

While serious scholars such as Umberto Eco gave a winking nod to the Smurf language in *Kant and the Platypus: Essays on Language and Cognition* (collected in 1997 and published in English two years later), screenwriters such as Richard Linklater and Richard Kelly had their deeply philosophical characters offer their thoughts of the nature of the Smurfs in *Slacker* (1991) and *Donnie Darko* (2001), respectively. Thanks to an episode of *South Park*, the film *Avatar* (2009) is colloquially called "Dances with Smurfs" because of the strong resemblance to the Smurfs that the Na'vi people bear in both color and lifestyle—a comparison *Avatar* writer/director James Cameron has publicly acknowledged and had some fun

with. *The Simpsons* depicted Lisa watching the very Smurf-ish cartoon called "The Happy Little Elves" and Adult Swim's parody program *Robot Chicken* featured numerous unflattering spoofs of the program, some of which featured members of the original Hanna-Barbera voice cast.

Saturday Night Live, which for decades has reflected popular culture back at us through the lens of comedy, has lampooned The Smurfs a number of times, the most laugh-inducing skits being their depiction of Smurfette as the star of her own reality show; their false advertisement for an "epic" Smurfs mini-series event that starred the likes of Sean Connery (actually comedian Darrell Hammond) as Papa; and a histrionic interpretation of *The Smurfs* theme by Celine Dion (Ana Gasteyer).

All the while, the original animated series remained in the periphery of the pop culture radar, shown in near perpetual reruns on the Cartoon Network and then on Boomerang, its "nostalgia" spin-off channel in America, and a variety of other networks worldwide. This allowed legions of preexisting fans to get their proper Smurf fix and new viewers to be introduced to the village.

vert et vert Schtroumpf," did deal with social issues like the culture war between French- and Dutch-speaking Belgians in their use of language. However, as the Smurfs were created and reached the pinnacle of their popularity during the Cold War, the fear of communism drove crackpots and intellectuals alike to see what they believed to be the seeds of socialism being planted in their children via Smurfs comics and cartoons. While some detractors were successful in getting their thoughts to the public during the run of the show, it would be through the Internet that their theories would spread globally, making their opinions accessible with the click of a mouse.

Some suggested that the Smurfs' very name indicated they were being used to indoctrinate children into communist socialism. The word S-M-U-R-F was claimed to be an acronym for Socialist Men Under Red Father (referring to the color of Communism, Karl Marx). Next came the fact that they live in a "commune," wherein each member of society performs a specific function that gives them their identity (Tailor Smurf makes clothes; Poet Smurf is a poet; and so on). Certain characters were ascribed particular symbolism—village leader Papa, for example, being a blue embodiment of both Marx and Lenin. Hefty and Brainy were compared to Lenin

followers Stalin and Trotsky, respectively (although it's never been documented that Trotsky was literally thrown out of Russia only to land on his head like Brainy was in numerous episodes of the series).

Other "clues" to the communist plot come from two of the more prominent Smurfs in the village: Handy and Farmer, who are often depicted as carrying a hammer and sickle, respectively, which when placed together comprise the emblem of the former Soviet Union. And then there was Gargamel, interpreted as an avatar for capitalism because one of his chief goals was to turn the Smurfs into gold!

In reality, conspiracy theorists thrive on seeing coincidences; none of this actually bears factual proof, and most of these interpretations can be easily dismissed. The "Socialist Men Under Red Father" weren't even born "Smurfs"; they were originally and still are called "les Schtroumpfs" in their native country. "Smurf" is a Dutch translation of a word that means absolutely nothing. The "typing" of the characters is basic cartoonist's shorthand that allows similar-looking characters to be distinguished from one another when participating in the narrative. Gargamel is a medieval sorcerer looking to make the Philosopher's Stone, and a Smurf is a key

LEFT | Gargamel's exact intentions for capturing the Smurfs may change, but his motives always amount to sheer vengeance for being bested by Papa in his first appearance.

ingredient in making that mythical substance. Much of fantasy-based literature features similar concepts and isn't making a sociopolitical statement either way.

Ultimately, if there was ever a truly political Smurfs story, it would be "Le Schtroumpfissime" (1964), translated as either "King Smurf" or "The Smurf King," in which a king is elected to watch over the Smurf Village in Papa's absence. Cowritten by Peyo and political anarchist Yvan Delporte, the acclaimed comic possibly presents an apolitical message of "absolute power can corrupt absolutely" as the story of the Smurf who becomes king in many ways mirrors that of Hitler as he's elected democratically and then becomes a totalitarian dictator. Eventually, the village is saved by the return of Papa Smurf, who through wisdom and earned authority restores normalcy to his Smurflings—proving there are systems that can and do work when leadership is based on reason and love.

Although some who have actually read it consider "Le Schtroumpfissme" to be, perhaps, the best of the comics, it's largely ignored by those trying to advance their own points made through weak connections and with perhaps no awareness of the decades of Smurfs material available to them.

RIGHT | Finished pages from the album *Le Schtroumpfissime* (1965) depicting a breakdown in the democratic process that allows for a despotic Smurf King to assume power in Papa's absence.

United Nations of Smurf

In 2005, the Smurfs did take a definitively political stance when the United Nations and I.M.P.S. teamed up to create a public service announcement for UNICEF, the UN children's fund. The shocking animated television commercial depicted the bombing of the Smurf Village set to the sound of Baby Smurf crying. Intended to raise consciousness of the effort to reform child soldiers in Burundi, the cartoon was created for "late-evening adult viewing" in Belgium and was scheduled to run after 9:00 PM to avoid viewing by younger audiences. However, the spot attracted a wealth of media attention and even went "viral" on the web, exposing the video to international audiences of all ages.

Since then, UNICEF and the Smurfs have teamed up for more youth-friendly promotions such as the sale of blank Smurf figurines that families could paint and then enter into a contest. A 2008 event was held in which larger versions of those figurines were decorated by celebrities and auctioned off to international bidders. In total,

more than 274,700 euros were raised to support UNICEF's educational programs.

It's also interesting to note that the United Nations' peacekeeping ground troops wear a shade of light blue, which has led them to be informally referred to as "Smurfs" by some of the military personnel and citizens who work along with them to provide support to free governments throughout the world.

in favor of UNICEF

Brave New Smurf

Though many fans throughout the world can argue that the Smurfs never really went away, no one can dispute the assertion that their overall visibility and availability have increased over the past few years. This was no more evident than in 2008 when they celebrated their 50th Anniversary.

In addition to a promotion that deposited handfuls of unpainted Smurfs in fifteen cities throughout Europe during a months-long promotional "Smurfday" tour, a forty-seven-foot-tall Smurf balloon was flown for the first time in the Macy's Thanksgiving Day Parade. The United States and Canada were privileged to receive a commemorative 50th Anniversary plush that included a "gold" Smurf and a reproduction of Peyo's first Smurf sketch. The Royal Belgian Mint issued a commemorative five-euro coin, a collectible limited to 25,000 pieces that had the Smurfs' 50th Anniversary logo emblazoned on the front.

Postage stamps, watches, and even celebratory figurines hit the market for collectors from all walks of Smurf fandom, and even the comic series itself honored its beginning by bringing back Johan and Pirlouit for a prequel to "La Flûte à Six Trous," "Les Schtroumpfeurs Noir."

OPPOSITE | A still from the 2005 UNICEF commercial in which the Smurf Village is bombed to the sounds of Baby crying.
RIGHT | The Smurf balloon takes its maiden voyage down the route of Macy's Thanksgiving Day Parade in November 2008.

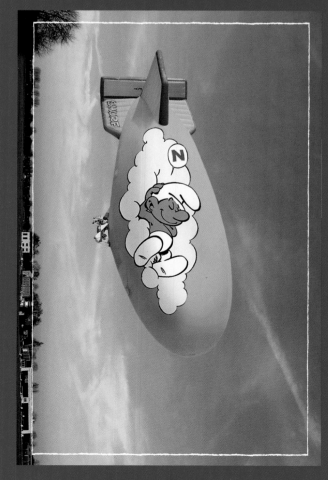

de Flûte" ("The Flute Smurfers"), which explored the story leading up to the events of the original 1958 adventure.

The Smurfs haven't stopped there. With appearances at the 2010 World Exposition in Shanghai, reprints of the original Smurfs comic albums in America and abroad (some featuring stories that have never been seen in print outside of the Belgian and French markets), new Smurfs comic albums being created annually, DVDs of the animated series seeing official release, and a major motion picture from Columbia Pictures/Sony Pictures Animation, the Smurfs are poised to continue smurfing well into the twenty-first century and beyond!

OPPOSITE | Promotional stills from the award-winning "Happy Smurfday" marketing campaign, and (BOTTOM RIGHT) a zeppelin soaring high above France. **RIGHT |** An assortment of the "Celebrity Smurfs" painted by noted international artists and auctioned off to benefit UNICEF. Contributors included Luxembourgian strongman Georges Christen; *Asterix* artist Albert Uderzo; and the Benetton family.

3(-D) APPLES HIGH

ON JUNE 17, 2010, a teaser trailer for an upcoming film hit the Internet, telling the world that "Smurf Happens," and for the first time, we saw what the Smurfs would look like if they were to spring from the two-dimensional universe of their comics and cartoons into our three-dimensional world. Although audiences would have to wait only another year to see the full story, the process of bringing Columbia Pictures'/Sony Pictures Animation's CGI/live-action hybrid film *The Smurfs* to the screen was for some a lifelong process, and for all involved, a labor of love that shows what would happen if our modern society got "Smurf'd."

More Than 2-Dimensional

Jordan Kerner was first introduced to the Smurfs in 1980, when his friend Brandon Tartikoff, then an executive at NBC, showed him the books from the animated series. Kerner instantly fell in love with the characters, and in a simple act of friendship, Tartikoff gave him a Smurfs comics album—starting a three-decades-long journey to bring *The Smurfs* to movie screens around the world.

After establishing a career as a film producer with a string of critically and commercially successful hits under his belt as diverse as *Fried Green Tomatoes* (1991), *The Mighty Ducks* (1992), *When a Man Loves a Woman* (1994),

George of the Jungle (1997), and *Charlotte's Web* (2006), Kerner began an active campaign to obtain the film rights to the Smurfs. Every year or so, he would send letters to the offices of Lafig Belgium, the company responsible for handling film and television rights, until he finally managed to convince Peyo's daughter Véronique and her team that he would stay true to the spirit and maintain the integrity of the original stories.

After years of development and what amounted to a false start at another studio, Michael Lynton, Chairman and Chief Executive Officer of Sony Pictures Entertainment, contacted Kerner about bringing the project to Sony. Lynton was raised in the Netherlands and had grown up a fan of the original Peyo albums that were regularly available to him as a child. According to Kerner, Sony rolled out the "blue carpet" for their meeting, at which both Lynton and Sony Pictures Co-chairman Amy Pascal ensured Kerner and Lafig Belgium that their property would be handled with care.

In the hands of Bob Osher, President of Sony Pictures Digital Productions, and Hannah Minghella, then President of Production at Sony Pictures Animation, The Smurfs film would transform from a purely animated

LEFT | (TOP) Raja Gosnell (at left) and Jordan Kerner (center) introduce Véronique and Nine Culliford to two "stuffies," the Smurfs' silicone stand-ins. (BOTTOM) Sony Pictures Digital Productions President Bob Osher chats on set with Hank Azaria's Gargamel. **OPPOSITE** | Early designs depicting the Smurfs' mushroom cottages. **PREVIOUS** | The Smurfs arrive in modern-day Manhattan.

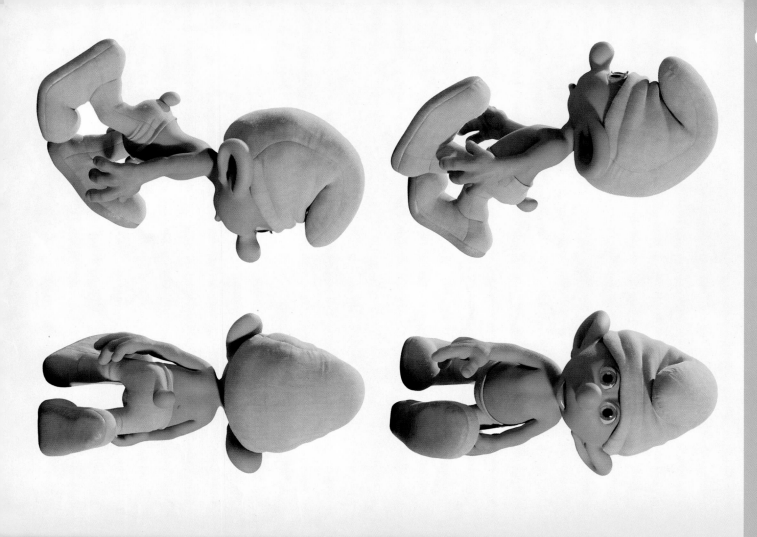

production to a hybrid of CGI and live action; a bold step forward for both the company and the Smurfs themselves. This development pleased Kerner, who in recent years had produced "hybrids" including *George of the Jungle* (1997), *Inspector Gadget* (1999), *Snow Dogs* (2002), and *Charlotte's Web* (2006).

Original still-frame concept drawings of the Smurfs were created and Sony Pictures Imageworks was charged with the process of fully rendering them as CG characters capable of realistic movement and believable interaction with live-action environments was begun.

Meanwhile, teams of writers including J. David Stern and David N. Weiss (both *Shrek 2*) and Jay Scherick and David Ronn (both *Zookeeper*) were enlisted to create a story in which the Smurfs were brought out of the comfortable environment of the Smurf Village circa the Middle Ages and into the quintessential "urban jungle" that is twenty-first-century Manhattan. Kerner worked side by side with Minghella to bring a real story to the core of the film along with all the Smurfs' signature comedy.

The story involves the Smurfs being accidentally transported into our world via a magical portal that only opens "once in a blue moon." Pursued by Gargamel, the Smurfs find themselves on an adventure that takes them from the Smurf Village into New York City, where

LEFT | A digital "turnaround" of Clumsy depicting the character from numerous angles. **OPPOSITE** | Raja Gosnell directs a scene set on the streets of New York City.

Raja Gosnell: A few words from *The Smurfs'* director

"The Smurfs are so intricately woven into people's childhoods; I was of course a bit reluctant to take on the great responsibility of making this film. However, in speaking to [producer] Jordan [Kerner], I realized we both agreed very much on what the tone and look of the movie should be. Knowing that I found a great ally in Jordan helped ease my initial trepidation . . . I know how much these little blue creatures mean to generations of kids and adults all over the world, and I wanted to give them a movie that they will enjoy for years to come. The midzone between honoring the source material and creating a compelling, feature-length movie is a challenging place to be. I like challenges, so hopefully we've created something that the longtime fans and new acquaintances will both enjoy.

"I think the idea of taking the Smurfs out of their enchanted forest and dropping them in the middle of a modern, urban jungle like present-day New York, offered us plenty of unique twists on the story of the Smurfs. Within that context, it was important to me to bring out the fun, adventurous element of the film—I wanted to show the Smurfs getting out of their comfort zone, let them run around NYC, and see what happens!"

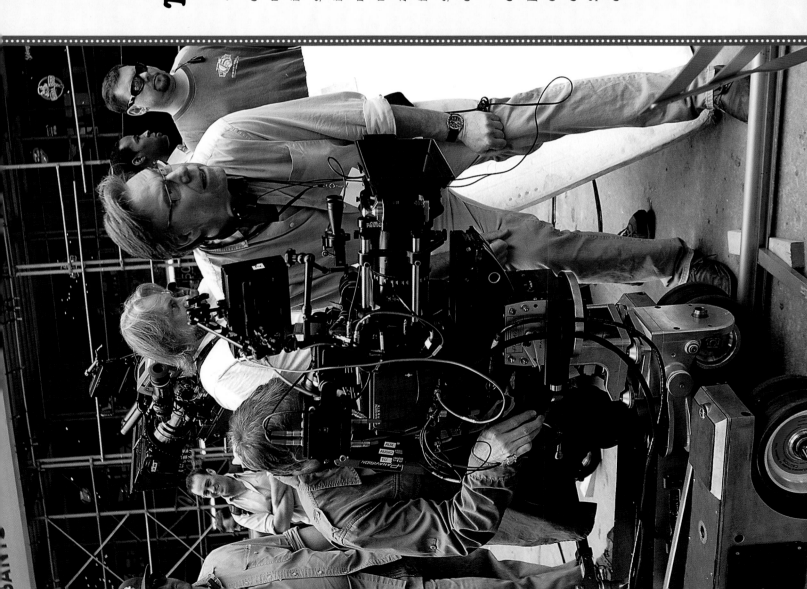

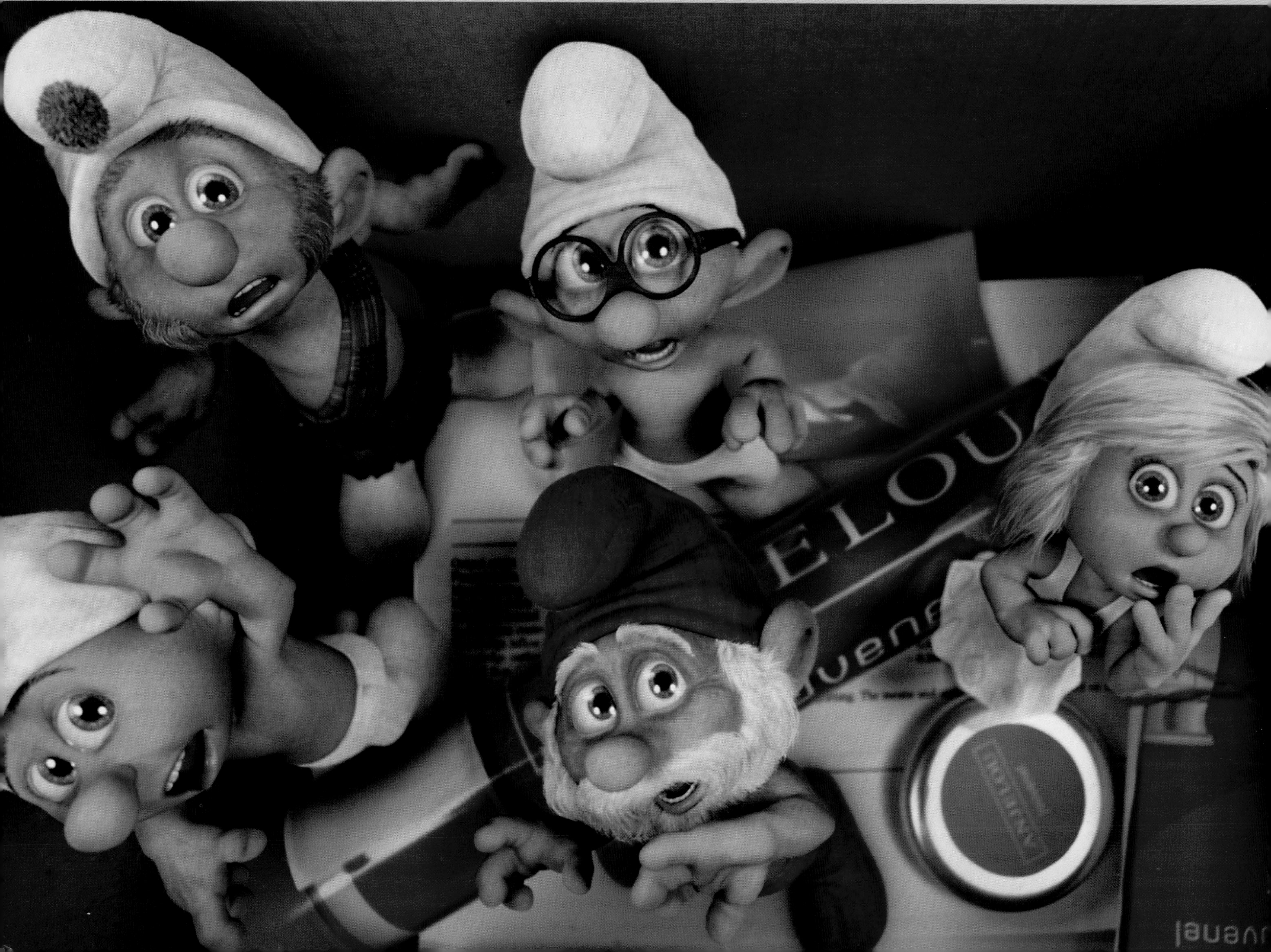
ELOU

they encounter strange locales including Times Square and Chinatown, and a toy store where they're mistaken for toys themselves. Aided in their quest to get home by expectant parents Patrick and Grace Winslow, the Smurfs manage to escape the clutches of Gargamel and of Odile Jouvenel, Patrick's boss, who has promised Gargamel riches and respect if he can provide a potion that can make aging people appear youthful again.

Along the way, Patrick and Grace learn about the power of magic, not only the kind that comes from potions and spells but the kind that comes from love and family, while the Smurfs pick up some life lessons of their own. At the heart of their story is Clumsy Smurf, who feels responsible for getting the Smurfs into their predicament through his own clumsy actions. However, as he helps lead and fight the Smurfs out of their problems, he learns that he is capable of so much more than just tripping over his own canoe-size feet. Ultimately, the lesson of the film is that whether or not someone's generally clumsy or brainy or grouchy, everyone is capable of proving that they're more than just one thing.

To helm the film Kerner sought out Raja Gosnell, who as the director of *Home Alone 3* (1997), *Never Been Kissed* (1999), *Big Momma's House* (2000), *Scooby-Doo* (2002) and its sequel, and *Beverly Hills Chihuahua* (2008) not only

OPPOSITE | A box full of Smurfs! **RIGHT** | (TOP) Actors Jayma Mays and Neil Patrick Harris as expectant parents Grace and Patrick Winslow. (BOTTOM) Clumsy gets animated while talking to the Winslows.

Who the Smurf is That?!?
MOVIE EDITION

The scope of The Smurfs film allowed for some other blue buddies to emerge from the sea of nameless white hats, and for some new human friends and enemies to join in the mix as well.

Gutsy Smurf, with an "act first, think about it later" attitude, plays the tough guy role in the film. His no-nonsense, gruff attitude is accented by a rich, rolling Scottish accent, provided by native Scotsman and Tony Award-winning actor Alan Cumming.

Panicky Smurf, a new character with a cameo in the film, is, as his name suggests, always fearful of what's going on around him. With Gargamel and Azrael always in hot pursuit of the Smurfs, how could he not be?

Patrick Winslow is the Smurfs' human guide and aide in the madcap modern world. A marketing executive for Anjelou Cosmetics and a first-time expectant father, Patrick must learn to navigate the choppy waters of balanc-ing a career and a family, and along the way learns from one of the best about what it takes to be a papa. He's played by Neil Patrick Harris.

Grace Winslow, Patrick's wife, is the first present-day person to encounter the Smurfs in our world. Played by Jayma Mays, the aptly named Grace helps her husband realize how truly special the Smurfs are and, in doing so, helps not only the blue gnomes but her marriage as well.

Odile Jouvenel, played by Sofia Vergara, is a former model and now chief executive of the cosmetics company Patrick works for. After an encounter with Gargamel in which the wizard's magic makes her mother appear twenty-five years younger, Odile becomes an unwitting accomplice in Gargamel's scheme to capture the Smurfs' essence and market it as a revolutionary beauty aid.

had experience in bringing a beloved cartoon property to the screen-but also understood how to handle the technical difficulties inherent in creating a live-action/CGI hybrid. "Raja was the perfect director," says Kerner. "He has great comedic abilities with a very adult sensibility. He is one of the smartest, most prepared and talented directors out there . . . and it helps that he has a little dark side in his comedy. We worked so closely together for it to be a real adult journey for the fans, but appropriate for the kids."

Throughout the principle photography process, Gosnell, Kerner, Visual Effects Supervisor Richard Hoover, Digital Effects Supervisor Daniel Kramer, and Animation Supervisor Troy Saliba worked with the cast and crew on making a film that would not only resonate emotionally with audiences but also look and feel as real as possible, despite the fact that some of the stars of the show would be added long after the cameras were packed away.

In order to aid the human actors (including Hank Azaria as Gargamel) in their performances, a series of tricks were used to create the illusion that the Smurfs were present for the entire sixty-three-day New York-based shoot. Silicone marionettes of each of the six lead Smurfs—Clumsy, Papa, Brainy, Grouchy, Smurfette, and

OPPOSITE | Gutsy is one of three Smurfs created especially for the 2011 film. **RIGHT |** (TOP) Silicone marionettes of the Smurfs were used on set in the CGI versions' stead. (BOTTOM) Hank Azaria's Gargamel is aided by a live-action Azrael, played by Mr. Krinkle (with assistance from Phil Tippett Studio).

...

Gutsy (who was created for the film)—were designed to scale and gave performers a physical presence to play off of. When possible, these "stuffies," as they were called, were maneuvered and voiced by on-set actors Sean Kenin and Minglie Chen (later to be replaced in post-production). When stuffies couldn't be used, the crew would sometimes employ laser pointers or moving pieces of filament wire to help establish consistent sight lines for the actors to follow.

Similarly, tricks had to be performed by the crew to produce a "Smurf's-eye" view of the world. To help along those lines, a special "Smurf Cam" was developed. Rudimentarily described by one filmmaker as being "like a paper towel tube with a lens attached," the camera was easily controlled and could be placed closer to the ground. The small wide-angle lens, necessary to keep it lightweight, greatly magnified the subjects it was photographing, making even the smallest household item seem huge—the way a Smurf would see it.

Once the footage was shot, the animators took over and an all-star voice cast was recorded performing the lines as they would be heard in the film. With gifted comedians such as Jonathan Winters (Papa), Fred Armisen (Brainy), and George Lopez (Grouchy), in

LEFT | (TOP) Raja Gosnell helps Neil Patrick Harris get acquainted with his little blue co-stars. (BOTTOM) Sofia Vergara and Hank Azaria film a scene in the heart of midtown Manhattan.

addition to the talent of celebrated young actor Anton Yelchin (as Clumsy) and singer Katy Perry in her first acting role (as Smurfette) providing expressive vocal tracks, animators were given a lot of material to use in fashioning the proper visuals to really make the characters come to life. (The actors were also video-recorded for the animators to reference.)

"There are thousands of nuances in a face," explains Troy Saliba. "The subtle movement of an eyelid can really make a performance." However, while it is Ms. Perry that we'll be hearing and to an extent seeing as Smurfette, the character will undeniably be the same one that Peyo created in 1966. "When you have recognizable talent voicing a character, some details are bound to slip in," says Saliba, to which Hoover adds, "But it's our job to make sure that our characters are the Smurfs."

Let's Get Physical!

Greetings, Smurfologists! It's time to put on our white lab coats and matching Phrygian caps to take a look at the evolution that our blue buddies underwent as a team of artists and animators at Sony Pictures Imageworks translated them from two-dimensional line drawings to

RIGHT | Legendary comedian Jonathan Winters lent his voice to Papa Smurf for the film. According Raja Gosnell: "Besides [Winters'] wonderful performance abilities and his uniquely resonant voice, he is also bringing a certain amount of authenticity to our movie, especially for the longtime Smurfs fans who grew up with him and the cartoon."

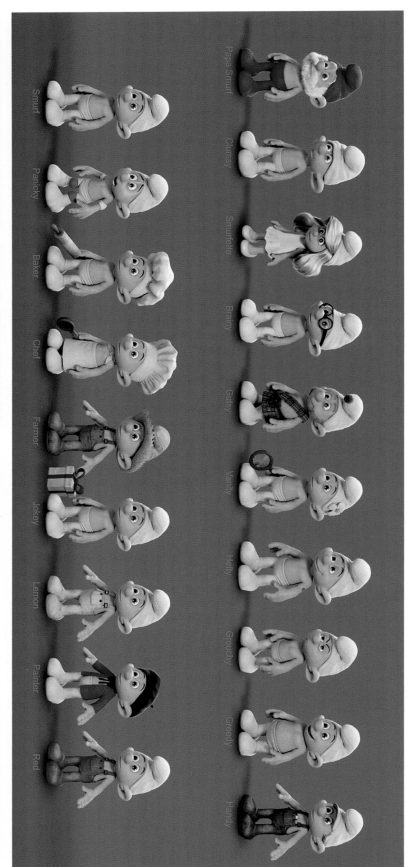

Smurf

Panicky

Baker

Chef

Farmer

Jokey

Lemon

Painter

Red

Papa Smurf

Clumsy

Smurfette

Brainy

Gutsy

Vanity

Hefty

Grouchy

Greedy

Handy

three-dimensional (almost living, breathing) beings for The Smurfs feature film.

In making the transition from page to screen, producer Kerner says that a lot of attention was paid to ensure that the characters never went too far afield: "We considered a lineup of characteristics from a simplistic line drawing to what ended up being too much detail—almost a troll. We think we found just the Smurfy balance."

Height: As we've previously discussed, the phrase "three apples high" was never a precise scientific measurement; previous artists in both the comic strips and cartoons have had the benefit of working in a purely illustrated medium where scale could expand or contract slightly to accommodate a specific panel or frame. The filmmakers, on the other hand, were confronted with the challenge of making their Smurfs interact with real environments and live actors, forcing them to determine a fixed measurement for their characters. After numerous tests, on various sized apples, of course, it was decided that 9 inches was the proper height (from the tips of their hats to the soles of their feet) at which to depict the Smurfs. If they were any larger, they would no longer appear to be the lovable leprechauns

OPPOSITE | (TOP) Digital character line-up. (BOTTOM) A look at the development of Papa Smurf's lab. **RIGHT** | Smurfette striking her dance-and-be-happy pose.

Skin: The transition to computer-generated "live" characters posed another interesting question: What does a Smurf's skin look like? In their original two-dimensional, flatly colored worlds, the answer was simple enough: It looks blue! However, Sony Pictures Imageworks was challenged with fleshing out the textural qualities of a Smurf's skin so that moviegoers could accept that the Smurfs were part of our world. "We had to take what we know of, or observe about, humans—like what happens when light penetrates the skin, and how does blood affect our coloration—and match that," notes the film's visual effects supervisor, Richard Hoover. "Wandering away from those qualities would make them seem alien."

After finding the right balance between the scientific and the magical, each Smurf's specific qualities (such as age and demeanor) had to be taken into account. For example, Papa Smurf's age would need to manifest itself in wrinkles and a rougher skin surface, while Smurfette would require an unblemished appearance and a lovely glow. For the movie, character designers and animators have chosen to express Brainy's relative youth through

with which the world was already familiar; any smaller and it would be too difficult for the Smurfs to properly relate to real-world objects and people.

LEFT | Movie stars Smurfette, Papa, Gutsy, and Clumsy, voiced by Katy Perry, Jonathan Winters, Alan Cumming, and Anton Yelchin, respectively. **OPPOSITE |** Smurf village sketches by Javier Ameijeiras and (UPPER FLAP) design by Bill Boes and painting by Gregory Hill.

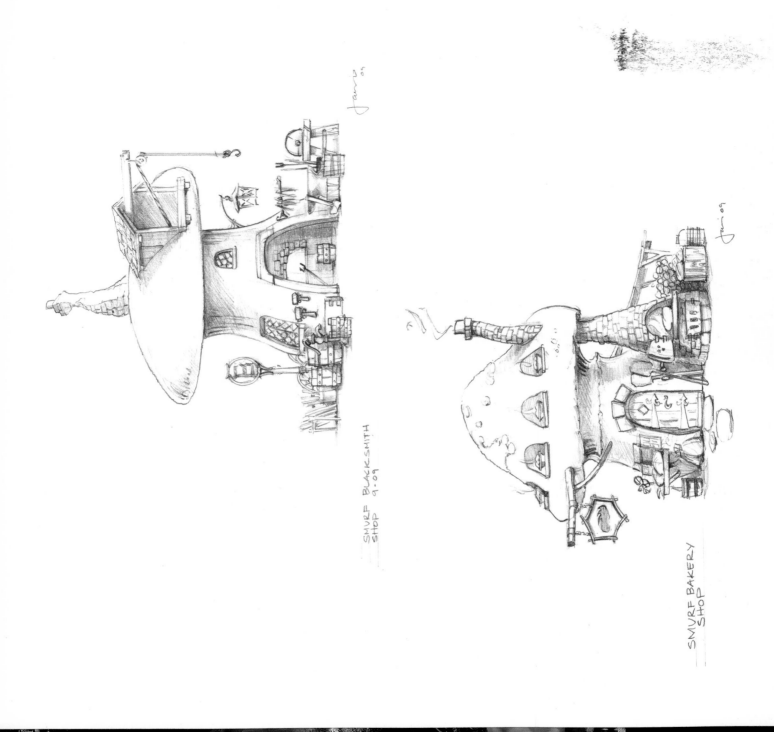

SMURF BLACKSMITH
SHOP 9-09

SMURF BAKERY
SHOP

the presence of freckles, allowing him to seem cute despite his continued role as a know-it-all.

Movement: By definition, the job of an animator is to make a character move. As previous attempts to bring the Smurfs into "our" world (through marionettes and puppetry) have proven, their original design, while adorable in its small stature and outsized features, defies some basic physical laws. Proportionally, an average person's height is equivalent to seven to nine times the size of his or her head, whereas a Smurf's head accounts for nearly one-third of his or her overall height!

To fully understand that, The Smurfs animation supervisor Troy Saliba offers the following perspective: "If a Smurf were to be as tall as an average human, then proportionally their head would be approximately three feet wide and their hands the size of snow shovels."

To build their digital models and properly animate them, the artists who worked on The Smurfs found that they had to slightly "tweak" Peyo's original concepts, but what they achieved were creatures that could realistically walk, hop, and hang from their fingers in our world. Thanks to the Sony animators, we now know that Smurfs can run up to 10 feet per second and have a vertical leap of 4 to 12 inches—instrumental in understanding how they always manage to avoid the grasp of Gargamel!

LEFT | (TOP) Brainy, Grouchy, and Gutsy up to something. (BOTTOM) Brainy is voiced with a youthful enthusiasm by Fred Armisen, a longtime cast member of *Saturday Night Live*.

OPPOSITE | Gusty and Clumsy making a smurfy breakfast.

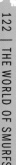

Afterword

As a small child, Véronique Culliford was always a little frightened of Gargamel: "He was the bad guy, and so mean to the Smurfs . . . who isn't afraid of the villain?"

So, imagine her surprise when she and her mother, Nine, were invited to the set of *The Smurfs* by producer Jordan Kerner and brought to a dressing room where, "We met the real Gargamel and saw him in all his wicked and evil glory!"

Kerner recalls having to gingerly escort the president of I.M.P.S. across the room to where the Smurfs' tormentor cackled, spoke, and offered his crooked hand in greeting. "You could see Véronique's eyes well up," recalls Kerner of the meeting. "She told me it was from the joy of seeing Peyo's character in the flesh, but I think some of it was seeing her childhood nightmares come to life!"

Nightmare or not, for Véronique the experience truly was a dream come true.

"This [movie] was such an important milestone in the Smurfs' life that I'd brought my mum along with me as her eightieth birthday present," Culliford recalls. "She was obviously at my dad's side every step of the way on the Smurf adventure, much more so than I or my brother. In a way, the Smurfs were their children in an imaginary world. . . . We were given a very warm Hollywood welcome (even though we were in New York!) and that's always been a dream, but this time it was for real!"

And of Gargamel, who after some makeup removal—and reassurance that he wouldn't try to turn the Cullifords into gold or eat them—revealed himself to be actor Hank Azaria, Véronique has only the most stellar of reviews:

"'Gargy-Hank' really is fantastic . . . There's only one thing I can say: I absolutely love his interpretation of this character that I've always known and grew up with. His movements were exactly as they'd always been in my imagination, and yet he also added a certain human vulnerability to the character that I'd never imagined but that fits him perfectly."

Adding that new layer of discovery and enjoyment to the property on the whole was, of course, the reason to bring *The Smurfs* to a different medium in a refreshing way for a whole new era.

"We had to do something different from the comic and the cartoons," explains Véronique, "but also be there to make sure the Smurfs stay the same . . . [The filmmakers] believed in *The Smurfs*, which enabled us to believe in them while they made the film."

"Our overall goal," notes Kerner, "was to depict not only what was on the page, but what Peyo's intentions were when he created the characters. They transcend all of our views of characters like these . . . his creations are enduring."

OPPOSITE | "Gargy-Hank" with Véronique and Nine Culliford.

Sources

"Applause Inc.—Company History." Funding Universe. N.p., n.d. Accessed October 24, 2010. http://www.fundinguniverse.com/company-histories/Applause-Inc-Company-History.html.

Barbera, Joseph. My Life in 'toons: From Flatbush to Bedrock in Under a Century. Atlanta, GA: Turner Publishing, Inc., 1994.

Burnett, Alan. E-mail interview. June 18, 2010.

Cendrowicz, Leo. "The Smurfs Are Off to Conquer the World—Again." Time, January 14, 2008. Accessed October 8, 2010. http://www.time.com/time/world/article/0,8599,1703303,00.html.

Culliford, Véronique. Personal interview. November 24, 2010.

Dayez, Hugues. Peyo l'enchanteur. Belgium: Editions Niffle, 2003.

"Dupuis: Peyo." Dupuis Publishing. Accessed October 26, 2010. http://www.dupuis.com/servlet/jphome?pgm=home&lang=UK.

"FAQ: Smurfs: What's it all about?" UNICEF, October 14, 2005. Accessed November 1, 2010. http://www.unicef.org/media/media_28772.html.

Folkart, Burt A. "Pierre Culliford, Created the Widely Popular Smurfs." Los Angeles Times, December 25, 1992. Accessed October 8, 2010. http://articles.latimes.com/1992-12-25/news/mn-2392_1-pierre-culliford.

Foray, June, Mark Evanier, and Earl Kress. Did You Grow Up With Me, Too? The Autobiography of June Foray. Albany, GA: BearManor Media, 2009.

Goodman, Martin. "Deconstruction Zone—Part 2: Dr. Toon continues to take on the deconstructionists about the things they read into classic cartoons." Animation World Network, March 10, 2004. Accessed October 28, 2010. http://www.awn.com/articles/drtoon/deconstruction-zone-part-2/page/1%2C1.

Guetel, Irina. "Die Schlümpfe feiern 50. Geburtstag." Die Berliner Literaturkritik, January 14, 2008. Accessed October 24, 2010. http://www.berlinerliteraturkritik.de/detailseite/artikel/die-schluempfe-feiern-50-geburtstag.html?tx_ttnews[backPid]=34&cHash=73+ce00e5960742 5d957ae249a160da9.

Hoover, Richard. Telephone interview. November 11, 2010.

Kerner, Jordan. Telephone interview. November 12, 2010.

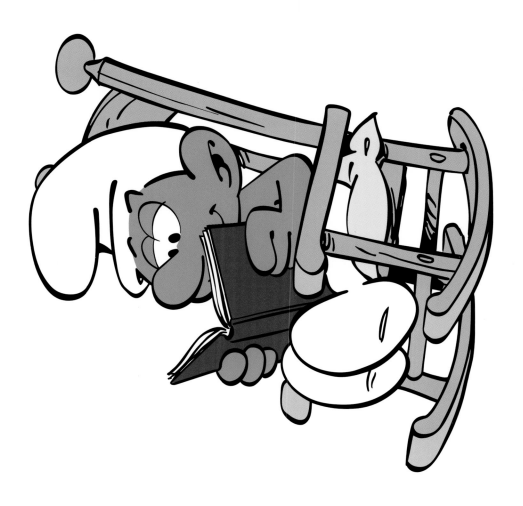

Kramer, Daniel. Telephone interview. November 17, 2010.

Lemelson-MIT Program. "Inventor of the Week Archive: Paul Winchell." Massachusetts Institute of Technology, September 2005. Accessed October 8, 2010. http://web.mit.edu/invent/iow/winchell.html.

Lenburg, Jeff. "The Smurfs." *The Encyclopedia of Animated Cartoons.* 3rd ed. New York, NY: Checkmark Books, 2008.

"Les Amis: Peyo." Franquin. March 2007. Accessed November 25, 2010. http://www.franquin.com/amis/peyo_amis.php.

Lindenberger, Jan. *More Smurf Collectibles: A Handbook and Price Guide.* Atglen, PA: Schiffer Publishing Ltd., 1998.

Lindenberger, Jan, and Joe Martone. *Smurf Collectibles: A Handbook and Price Guide.* Atglen, PA: Schiffer Publishing Ltd., 1996.

Losonsky, Joyce and Terry. *Unauthorized Guide to Smurfs Around the World.* Atglen, PA: Schiffer Publishing Ltd., 1999.

Mansour, David. "Smurfs." *From Abba to Zoom: A Pop Culture Encyclopedia of the Late 20th Century.* Kansas City, MO: Andrews McMeel Publishing, 2005.

Mechem, Alan. E-mail interview. October 26, 2010.

Minghella, Hannah, and Bob Osher. Telephone interview. November 5, 2010.

Parkes, Stephen. E-mail interview. October 26, 2010.

Saliba, Troy. Telephone interview. November 11, 2010.

"Smurf Sign Language—Sign Language Symbol for Butterfly." Blue-buddies.com. Accessed October 8, 2010. http://bluebuddies.com/Smurfs_Smurf_Sign_Language.htm.

"Smurfiversary: Interview with Heather Hendershot and Thierry Culliford," by Brooke Gladstone, On the Media, NPR: WNYC, February 29, 2008. Accessed October 8, 2010. http://www.onthemedia.org/transcripts/2008/02/29/07.

Winterman, Denise. "They're Smurf a fortune." *BBC News Magazine,* October 24, 2008: n. pag. Accessed October 24, 2010. http://news.bbc.co.uk/2/hi/uk_news/magazine/7686070.stm.

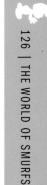

Photo by Michael Piñeiro

About the Author

Matt. Murray earned his BFA in film, television, and radio production from NYU. A former president and the first executive director of New York's Museum of Comic and Cartoon Art, he curated the popular "Saturday Morning" exhibit and crafted events and programming such as the year-long retrospective "1986: The Year That Changed Comics." He contributed to and was interviewed for the "I Smurf the Smurfs" documentary on The Smurfs Season 1, Volume 2 DVD and has served as the "Smurf Consultant" on Papercutz' series of Smurfs graphic novels. In addition to his Smurfology work, Murray is an actor, a pop culture blogger, and a collector of original comic, cartoon, and animation artwork. He lives in Bethlehem, Pennsylvania, with his cat (not named Azrael).

THE AUTHOR WISHES TO THANK

Noreen C. & Stephan G. Murray; Phoebe, the "Kids," Figs, & All Murray's Great and Small; Allan Dorison, Jennifer Babcock, Jared Gniewek, Ken Wong, and everyone from the ol' S.A.C.; Papercutz Graphic Novels: Management and Staff of Starters Riverport; Alan Burnett; Veronique Culliford (and Nina); Richard Hoover; Jordan Kerner; Raja Gosnell; Daniel Kramer; Alan Mechem; Hannah Minghella; Bob Osher; Stephen Parkes; Diane Pfeifer; Troy Saliba; b&m!, Lafig Belgium, Sony Pictures Consumer Products, and Sony Pictures Animation; and anyone who made this experience as easy as possible for everyone involved. Smurf Life!

An extra smurfy shout-out goes to Jim Salicrup for being a mentor, entertainer, friend, and a great late-night dinner companion during some interesting times. Thank you for everything.

If you're still reading along, the answer is: Smurf.

Image Credits

Culliford family archives: pages 10, 12, 13, 14, 15, 16, 18, 22 (right), 28 (top), 30, 33, 34, 35, 43, 51, 53, 54, 57, 67, 68; © I.M.P.S.: pages 3, 4, 5, 6, 22 (left), 23, 25, 26, 28 (bottom), 51, 61 (bottom), 62, 64 (background), 65, 70, 73, 76, 77, 78, 79, 80, 81, 82, 83, 84, 85, 86, 87, 88, 89, 90, 91, 96, 97, 98, 102, 103, 124, 125, 126, © I.M.P.S./Dupuis: pages 17, 19, 20, 21, 24, 29, 36, 37, 39, 40 (bottom), 42, 99; © I.M.P.S./Papercutz: pages 27, 38, 56, 74, 75; © TVA/Dupuis/I.M.P.S.: page 32; © Kellogg's/I.M.P.S.: page 40 (top); © Belvision/Dupuis/I.M.P.S. : pages 44, 45, 46, 47; © AB Productions/ I.M.P.S.: page 50; © Wallace-Berrie/ I.M.P.S./ Courtesy of Matt. Murray: pages 52 (right), 66; © UNICEF/I.M.P.S.: page 100; © Eric Preau/Sygma/Corbis: pages 48, 69; © Hanna-Barbera/Courtesy of Everett Collection: pages 58 (bottom left), 60 (top and middle); Courtesy of Alan Mechem: pages 41 (all), 52 (left), 58 (top), 94 (top and bottom left), 95; Courtesy of Ross Gordon: page 94 (bottom right); Courtesy of Matt. Murray: pages 56 (right), 58 (bottom right), 61 (top), 63, 72 (all); Courtesy of Everett Collection: page 59 (top); Courtesy of Macy's Inc.: page 101; ™ & © Hanna-Barbera. (s11). Courtesy of Warner Bros. Entertainment Inc.: pages 55, 56 (right), 58 (top), 61 (top), 63, 72; Photo by FPG/Getty Images: page 64 (top); Courtesy of Sony Pictures Animation: pages 104, 108, 110, 111 (bottom), 112, 115, 116, 117, 120, 121; Photos by K.C. Bailey, courtesy of Columbia Pictures Industries/Sony Pictures Animation: pages 106, 109, 111 (top), 113, 114, 122.

Copyright © 2011

SMURFS & ™ 2011 Licensed through Lafig Belgium/IMPS www.smurf.com. The Smurfs, the Movie © 2011 Columbia Pictures Industries Inc. and Sony Pictures Animation Inc. All rights reserved.

Editor: Wesley Charlotte Royce

Cataloging-in-Publication Data has been applied for and may be obtained from the Library of Congress.

ISBN: 978-1-4197-0072-9

The World of Smurfs is produced by becker&mayer!, Bellevue, Washington. www.beckermayer.com

Design: Rosebud Eustace
Editorial: Amy Wideman
Image Research: Shayna Ian
Production Coordination: Shirley Woo
License Acquisition: Josh Anderson

The text of this book was composed in
Joanna MT, ITC Franklin Gothic, and Cooper Black.

Published in 2011 by Abrams Image, an imprint of ABRAMS. All rights reserved. No portion of this book may be reproduced, stored in a retrieval system, or transmitted in any form or by any means, mechanical, electronic, photocopying, recording, or otherwise, without written permission from the publisher.

Printed and bound in China.
10 9 8 7 6 5 4 3 2 1

Abrams Image books are available at special discounts when purchased in quantity for premiums and promotions as well as fundraising or educational use. Special editions can also be created to specification. For details, contact specialsales@abramsbooks.com or the address below.

ABRAMS
THE ART OF BOOKS SINCE 1949

115 West 18th Street
New York, NY 10011
www.abramsbooks.com